MECHANICS-
MERCANTILE
❦
LIBRARY.

Arthur F Mathews '06

The Sights Along the Harbor

WESLEYAN POETRY

Other Wesleyan Titles by Harvey Shapiro

Battle Report: Selected Poems, 1966
This World, 1971
The Light Holds, 1984
National Cold Storage Company: New and Selected Poems, 1988
Selected Poems, 1997
How Charlie Shavers Died and Other Poems, 2001

Also by Harvey Shapiro

The Eye, 1953
Mountain, Fire, Thornbush, 1961
Lauds, 1975
Lauds & Nightsounds, 1978
A Day's Portion, 1994
Poets of World War II (editor), 2003

The Sights
Along the Harbor

New and Collected Poems

Harvey Shapiro

Wesleyan University Press
Middletown, Connecticut

Published by Wesleyan University Press,
Middletown, CT 06459
www.wesleyan.edu/wespress

Printed in the United States of America

5 4 3 2 1

Library of Congress Cataloging-in-Publication Data
Shapiro, Harvey, 1924–
The sights along the harbor : new and collected poems / Harvey Shapiro.
    p.   cm. — (Wesleyan poetry)
Includes index.
ISBN-13: 978-0-8195-6795-6 (cloth : alk. paper)
ISBN-10: 0-8195-6795-7 (cloth : alk. paper)
I. Title. II. Series.
PS3537.H264S56   2006
811'.54—dc22   2005021349

To the memory of

Dorothy Cohen and

Jacob J. Shapiro

Contents

From *Mountain, Fire, Thornbush,* 1961, 33

From *Battle Report,* 1966, 45

From *This World,* 1971, 63

From *The Light Holds*, 1984, 133

From *National Cold Storage Company*, 1988, 165

From *A Day's Portion*, 1994, 177

Author's Note

I began writing poetry seriously after World War II, partly as a result of my experience in that war. The earliest poems in this book appeared in magazines in the early fifties; the most recent poems were completed in November of 2004. That span of time accounts, in small measure, for the changes in style the interested reader will find here. In compiling this book, I have omitted some poems from previously published books because they no longer interest me for one reason or another: they repeat what I think is better said in other poems, or, with the passage of time, they seem irrelevant to my main concerns. The poems included here constitute the body of my work as I now see it. I count myself a lucky survivor and am pleased, as I hope readers will be, with what I've done with my time.

—BROOKLYN, AUGUST 2005

Acknowledgments

Poems from the following sections are reprinted with the permission of the original publishers.

Poems from *Lauds & Nightsounds* (SUN) used by permission of the publisher are: "Through the Boroughs," "Notes at 46," "Riding Westward," "For the Yiddish Singers in the Lakewood Hotels of My Childhood," "In Brooklyn Harbor," "'Jesus, Mary I Love You Save Souls,'" "For the Sparrows on New Year's Morning," "Distances," "True," "Saul's Progress," "Bringing Up Kids," "Veteran," "Every Day," "Muse Poem," "In the Room," "Arriving," "Montauk Highway," "A Notebook," "In Our Day," "How Differences Arise," "Janis," "Adaptation of a First-Grade Composition," "In Fear of Failure," "For the Year's End," "City Portrait," "A Gift," "Like a Beach," "August," "Musical Shuttle," "Tight Like That," "The Bridge," "Incident," "47th Street," "In the Synagogue," "Brooklyn Gardens," "Nightsounds," "Domestic Matters," "Cry of the Small Rabbits," "For the Zen Master Skateboarding Down Independence Pass," "Muffdiving on the Upper West Side," "O Seasons," "Ancient Days," "1976," "Portrait," "Poets & Comics," "The Realization," "The Old Wife Speaks," "Vacation Poetry," "After Dark," "Lines," "The Intensity," "Happiness in Downtown Brooklyn," "From a Chinese Master," and "Ditch Plain Poem."

Poems reprinted from *A Day's Portion* © 1994 by Harvey Shapiro, by permission of Hanging Loose Press.

Some of the new poems have appeared in the following publications: *The Saint Ann's Review, The New Criterion, Boulevard, Natural Bridge, Smartish Pace, The Forward, Hanging Loose, Open City, Present Tense* (Hanging Loose Press, 2004), and *Lasting: Poems on Aging* (Pima Press, 2005).

New Poems

DESK

After my death, my desk,
which is now so cluttered,
will be bare wood, simple and shining,
as I wanted it to be in my life,
as I wanted my life to be.

TO NATURE

Sun gilding each lance-like pine needle.
One needs to have a proper attitude of respect
as a Jew only recently out of his village in Russia
would have had when he first ventured
from the Lower East Side on to broad Fifth Avenue.
My eyes are wide. I lift my cap.

CATHEDRAL

I went out
and this thought rose
before me like a great cathedral
and it said:
Transcendence. Transcendence.
Or at least
try a bit harder.

IN JAPAN

I put my empty glass
on the top of Mt. Fuji
and go to sleep.

IN A BAD TIME

1
Raphael, the affable arch-angel,
he's the one I need.
I have these questions to put to him:
Why has the music in my head
and heart stopped? What terrible
thing have I done? Explain
it to me gently.

2
Who created you? Jacob J. Shapiro
and Dorothy Cohen. They created me,
and my dead sister, Annette, and my
younger brother, Allan. Who will uncreate
you? Impossible to predict just now
but my money is on pastrami.

THE LIBRARIAN

I thought I was in love with a librarian
in Lynn, Massachusetts.
She had red hair, a freckled face,
was thin. That's about all I remember
except that summer, in Cummington,
I wrote a poem for her that, surprisingly,
in view of the barrenness of the experience,
seems to have full-throated ardor, whereas
women I have explored for years
have left me with only a few anecdotes.
So this is the gift of youth, I say to myself,
of ignorance and delusion.
It is never given again.

REQUIEM

Leo, the way the girls used to strut
down the ramp from the ferry into Goldie's
on Ocean Beach, Fire Island, summers ago.
It was like something out of a musical,
whose tunes, I bet, you're still humming to yourself in death.

RAIN ON SCUTTLE HOLE ROAD

The rain on Scuttle Hole Road
seen through the windshield
in strings and clots illuminated
by the headlights. She was talking
about Bush's relationship
with Putin. I said, I didn't know
they were having one. Would you bomb
Iraq? Actually, I'd bomb almost
anyone these days of seeing everything
in its extenuating global context—
like sheer hatred, I suppose,
the kind that charges up your voice
when you say, I have to use fuck
when I talk to you.

BUS RIDE

And now the bus, on an elevated highway,
rises above Queens, that borough of the dead.
The family all ride with me, into the 21st Century,
which, as it turns out, looks nothing like
the World of the Future displayed in Queens
at the General Motors Exhibit in the 1939 World's Fair
but is, in fact, much closer to the world

of the Old Testament with its warring tribes,
bloodletting and confusion. A world I absorbed
in Hebrew School in pre-adolescence and carry
with me into the familiar dark.

THE NEWS

The Muslims in London are screaming,
Kill the filthy Jews.
I heard it on the BBC.
I agree, and call my brother
in Israel to give up the settlements.
Also, while he's at it,
what about the grandchildren?
Maybe the world is getting ready for another
big bonfire. You bring the marshmallows.
I'll bring the Jews.

GOD POEM

Nobody does silence as well as God.
He fills whole cathedrals with it,
store-front churches and synagogues.
We once believed in the music of the spheres
but now we hear silence—static and silence.
It can be overwhelming—the way God
was said to be overwhelming in the old books:
when he talked to Job, for example,
or when he instructed Moses on
what plagues to deal out
or when he described to Noah just
what he was going to do, and then did it.
Better to be nourished by the silence.

COMMENTARY

Bereshit, the Hebrew scholars once
translated as "In the beginning"
thereby foretelling
"In the end" and maybe bringing
death into the world and all our woe
is now translated as "At the beginning"
or "When in the beginning"—
a bit blurred, not the knife-edge
of sunrise but an ongoing process
that, maybe, doesn't
have to end but is infinitely expandable
like the universe itself
or the mind of God, or the text
on which the mind of God is splayed
like stars across the firmament.

ACCORDING TO THE RABBIS

According to the rabbis,
when God asks Adam, Where are you?
He's not looking for information.
He wants Adam to consider where he is in his life,
where he is NOW and where he intends to be.
I could say that I'm on a bus, headed for New York,
but that would be frivolous. I could say
that I'm in the middle of a dark wood,
that I'm always in the middle of a dark wood.
But that would be despair.

THE GENERATIONS

His son stood, holding and rocking the baby,
swaying back and forth, combined
with a little sideways shuffle,

which he had never done in shul,
since he never went to shul,
though his father had and his father had,
so the prayer that bound them all
was still being said.

ADAM

It is possible Adam
was bored in paradise,
the leafy green settling
in his mind like fog.
I have a taste for something
else, he thought, but what?

IN ATHENS

Is everything we say
heard with a double meaning
by the gods, who know
how our story ends, the way
the audience in Athens knew
how the story ends and could feel
the knife-edge in even the most
ordinary utterance of Oedipus?

BROOKLYN WALK

The shellfish at the bottom of New York Harbor
live populous and untouched lives
among the poisons of the last century.
I think of them as I set off
for the pier beside the Brooklyn Bridge
to see the Chinese brides in their gowns and flowered hair.

Huge slug-like white limos in rows await them
while the cameras roll. Across the harbor,
as I walk, I see Ellis Island and imagine
my mother and father, both young,
both just arrived, viewing me from there
along with the other sights along the harbor.
Down the hill I go, past the enormous letters
of the WATCHTOWER, citadel
of the Jehovah's Witnesses, a religion
born in the New World. At the pier,
sculpted into the black grillwork facing
the Manhattan skyline, are phrases
from Whitman's "Crossing Brooklyn Ferry."
I sometimes stand before "scallop-edg'd waves."
Or if I'm there at sunset
"drench with your splendor me."

READING OUTDOORS

My mind keeps wandering into hell,
irrelevance and hell, or at least
the meagerly furnished antechamber
with its commemorative pots—the time
you did this, the time you did that.
And then you try to find your way
back to the page, and the next
minute you're dozing. Better
to watch the copters and gulls,
anything moving out there,
anything that catches light.

KUANON

Lots of eye-candy on the streets
of New York, these days, in all flavors.
I seem to favor the slim Asiatics,

shining black hair, masked faces
I can't begin to see into, though I know
they are not there to represent merciful Kuanon
but are thinking about their jobs or boyfriends
or children. Still, they are in my landscape
and, I think, maybe to remind me
of a woman I might have married just after the war,
Japanese-American and very kind to me
and I was loutish, selfish, interested only
in my own pleasure, to use her beauty
only for my own pleasure. Well, these women
are beautiful too, spaced along the sidewalk
like bodhisattvas. I would follow them
anywhere, deep in my spiritual self.

FIVE DAYS IN PARIS

1. Madeline

"Madeline n'existe pas en France"
the lady in the toy shop
in the heart of Paris said to me.
I was looking for a present for my *petite fille*,
Amelia, who loves Madeline.
How can I explain to her
the great absence that now
hangs over this city—the city
of Baudelaire and Apollinaire but
not of Madeline, who like so many
is exiled from where she most belongs.

2. In the Louvre

I like my miracles in the living room
as in this 15th-century Dutch Annunciation.
The lady puts her book down for a moment
in deference to the angel, who is
trying to tell her something, while at the same time

struggling with his wings that are
too large for the small, well-furnished room.
The colors are the key to everything.
They are so rich and bright
as they might have been in the beginning
or as the painter believed them to be
in this beginning. They light up the room
for the lady as this small painting,
for a moment, lights up a world.

3. Paris

Just another ancient city that killed
its Jews. No, try again. This lit jewel
of a city—its ironwork, cathedrals, stones,
its power to hurt the heart with so much beauty.
"Transcendence isn't his line of work"
said today of Simenon in Le Figaro.
Maigret, of course, would want
always to be in these streets.

4. Cluny

A woman is about to fuck a unicorn
in the middle of Paris. As my mother
used to say, it takes all kinds.

5. Tourist

I stand on the Pont de la Tournelle
and see floating toward me
over the moiling Seine,
flying buttresses in advance,
stately Notre Dame
into my astonished heart.

NIGHT IN THE HAMPTONS

Across the table, he watches her stick
her tongue up the man's ass. It goes deeper
as the dinner progresses—You were so
great on Charlie Rose, she says—he thinks
soon she will follow her tongue, up and up,
and disappear. But it doesn't happen.
The man's wife is cooly blonde and oblivious.
It is night in the Hamptons, over chopsticks,
waiting for the imperial war to begin. He
notices she has almost stopped slurping.
Soon the surf and the stars can move in.

CHANCE MEETING

Just family trouble, said Lear,
and what's new with you?

TRAIN TRIP

Going to Croton-Harmon
I don't look at "The Lordly Hudson"
though I can hear Paul Goodman
on the phone explaining why—
I had asked him why—he had left
the stage of the Quaker Meeting House
in tears, as the actors in the audience
began to shout, "Paradise Now, Paradise Now,"
banging their seats in unison, and
Ben Hecht's lovely blonde daughter, Jenny,
(long since dead of an overdose) climbed
down from her box seat to liberate the stage.
And then Norman Mailer in his phony southern
sheriff voice tried to and couldn't quiet the crowd.
Why? Because Paul said he had been Judith Malina's

therapist and now she was treating him terribly,
in public, at what was to have been a civil
discussion of The Living Theater and blossomed
instead into the gorgeous fascism of the left.

JUMP SHIP

If you can't say what you mean,
then you might as well jump ship.
Like yesterday, even after
I had climbed the mountain,
I could not put Vermont together.
Spiritual heights are a downer
these days when what I need
is a jolt of real blue, and what I get
are piles of brown leaves
sliding by at a walker's pace.
Incremental evidence that something
is changing or is spooked and fleeing.

ONE DAY

Some lonely bird's insistence
that the sun rise.

The way mankind believes in a golden age
he believes in a time he had talent.

Thunder says the storm is approaching.
The chairs sit on the deck, waiting for rain.

The umber nipples
of the women of Lucca.

A bird moves through space
as if it contained corridors.

Jays jab at the world.
Their blue is not happy.

Children love dinosaurs because
if dinosaurs existed, we would not.

In his dream, he came to his dead friend
for help. His friend said, take my place.

His goal was obscurity
but he kept blundering into sense.

FROM AN AUTOBIOGRAPHY

He was riding his bike down Central Avenue,
coming from the public library in Far Rockaway
where he had been memorizing a poem by Edgar Allan Poe
and as he pedalled through the towns
of Inwood, Lawrence, Cedarhurst to his family's
apartment across from the train station
in Woodmere, he recited to himself hypnotically:

> I was a child and she was a child
> In that kingdom by the sea.
> But we loved with a love that was more than love,
> I and my Annabel Lee.

It occurs to him now that he had been reading Poe
because of his mother. He had
never seen her read poetry or heard her speak of it
but she had named his younger brother
Allan Edgar after the poet.
Maybe at Washington Irving High School
where she had gone each day with a clove
of garlic tied around her neck to ward off
sickness and the evil eye, some teacher,
in a momentary way, had caught her up
in one of Poe's poems. Or maybe

Poe represented poetry to her
and poetry upward mobility, she
being out of Russia and the poverty-strewn streets
of the Lower East Side. But how
to disentangle upward mobility
from the reach for something beautiful—
something to hand a child, as if to say,
Outside this apartment there is a beautiful world.
But we never spoke of beauty or of poetry.

TELLING THE MUSE WHAT IT'S LIKE AFTER 70

You try to simulate the feeling of something catching.
You believe it has caught.
A small fire begins to warm your ribs.
Not enough to launch a rocket.
No, more like a paper fire with a few sticks
in a rusty ash can
on a street corner of a winter night
towards which men, down-and-out, stretch their hands.

SKY

Winter sky netted in bare branches.
I may be wasting God's time.

Rudy walked into a pond.
Sarah put a noose around her neck.
Powdered snow drifts from the trees.

On the long walk along the harbor
I try to tell if my life is
ending happily or not
but everything merges in the quiet.

Brilliant winter sun.
How the pine needles shine.

PAYBACK TIME

What is that cruel food
and who hunts it through every vein
of my body. That cruel food
is pain and who fattens on it,
I ask, without paranoia, looking around me.
Well, it is payback time and the energy I have
withdrawn from the universe days and nights
without reckoning needs to be converted
into countable coin. And pain fills the till
as well as anything. I had thought art
would buy me out of this. I had thought
energy converted into poetry paid back
whoever or whatever it is that collects
and collects until collection's done.

HIS STORY

He runs his mind
back over his life
and he can't make out
the story, can't tell
if the story has a point,
doesn't know if he has come
to safe harbor, or is still
on the open sea. Meanwhile,
he enjoys the sun and the wind
on his face, and the sea spray.

FOR GABRIEL PREIL

"The grey sunken cunt of the world,"
wrote Joyce about Palestine.
Words for Leopold Bloom, who
preceded the Zionist experiment,
happy padding through Dublin
having his own Jewish experience—
Dawn in the Diaspora—looking
a little like Gabriel Preil, I imagine,
the Hebrew bard of the Bronx (long departed).
May his soul be as a sail on Lake Kinneret
in the blue immensity of time.

MADONNA DOES KABBALAH

Pornography of the spirit
is fast replacing pornography
of the body, as Madonna
does her Kabbalah, and the husks
of what was living
cluster around her feet.

SERIOUSLY

What music is it you think
you still have in you?
What stories haven't you told?
When they bring down the curtain
you will be in the middle of what speech?

ON THE STREET

You hear what I'm saying?
You know what I mean?

Nobody hears what you're saying.
Nobody knows what you mean.

THE NEED

The deep need to be absolutely
alone in his life so that he can
understand it.

What does that mean—
to understand one's life?
Maybe to feel for the first time
some connection between boy and man.

He needs to be in his life
the way he needs to be with a woman.

He is trying to describe
a constant, unappeasable hunger.

THIS WORLD, THAT WORLD

Standing by the Brooklyn Bridge,
watching the flow of the East River,
remembering Kyoto, water over stone.

Skeletons and hungry ghosts
ride the Lexington Avenue Express.

I have no memory of my entrance into this world
and will have no memory of my departure.

COLORS

In April's late afternoon sun
the colors of the world deepen.
If it could be done, I would sit now
in Kyoto, by myself, looking out
at the raked stones, the sparse green,
of a Zen garden. Years ago, before
they closed it for renovation,
a renovation that has never ended,
you could sit that way in Brooklyn,
in the Brooklyn Botanic Garden's
own Zen garden. I would go there
late Saturday afternoons with my younger
son, and I would understand what peace
is possible in this world. I think
that was a time I may have taught him
something. I who have been so niggardly
in instruction. And now this rich color
seeps into my day, and maybe all my days.

LANDSCAPE

Trees that in their silence uphold silence.

THE USES OF POETRY

This was a day when I did nothing,
aside from reading the newspaper,
taking both breakfast and lunch by myself
in the kitchen, dozing after lunch
until the middle of the afternoon. Then
I read one poem by Zbigniew Herbert
in which he thanked God for the many beautiful
things in this world, in a voice so absurdly
truthful, the entire wrecked day was redeemed.

EXPLAINING IT

The way a serial killer gets horny for death
The way the Scorpion Kings play their music
The way Coleridge shakes his big gall-drops
The way Alec Baldwin picks up the cop's dentures
The way a hurricane streams into our Atlantic coast
The way my life keeps looking for language.

NIGHTS

Drunk and weeping. It's another night
at the live-in opera, and I figure
it's going to turn out badly for me.
The dead next door accept their salutations,
their salted notes, the drawn-out wailing.
It's we the living who must run for cover,
meaning me. Mortality's the ABC of it,
and after that comes lechery and lying.
And, oh, how to piece together a life
from this scandal and confusion, as if
the gods were inhabiting us or cohabiting
with us, just for the music's sake.

AT THE SEMINAR

Who was the writer of *Job*
who made up those speeches God speaks
so convincingly we think it is God—
"And the morning stars sang together."
Who had that audacity
and then lived to tell the tale?
When we talk about the book,
in New York, some years later,
we question God's meaning and motives
as if he were real and not just
a character energized by a word-drunk

celestial-high writer, on assignment possibly,
at a café table in Nineveh or Tel Aviv.

THE OLD POET SUMS UP

Too many women,
not enough thought.

This is what the wind said to me
as I sat by myself under the pine trees:
Everything you assume will happen, will happen,
and all of it will amaze you.

I thought I was shouting
but to the world
my lips were hardly moving.

My dreams begin to entertain me.
I can't anticipate where they will take me.
The wind tugs at my door.

I see I have entered Homer's poem,
sitting with the old men on the city wall,
waiting for a look at Helen.

Once I spoke about nothingness
though I had never experienced it.
Now I begin to know it
as I know my mouth, my teeth, my tongue.

THE SUN'S CLEAR LIGHT

The sun's clear light
can be deadly. So it was
for many during the war,
so it is for many now.
Yet we count it a blessing
no more dangerous than life.

FROM

The Eye

1953

SEASCAPE

The glazed day crumbles to its fall
Upon the tiny rout of fishing
Boats. Gulls convey it down,
Lengthening their cries that soon
Will rake the evening air; while some,
Silhouetted on a strand
In a jumbled line of target ducks,
Watch as ebb tide drains the bay.

From a rotted log upon
The shore, like the other beached
Mutations, shell and weed, I wait
For Highland Light to cast its eye.

July unhives its heaven
In a swarm of stars above my head.
And at my feet, flat to the water
That it rides, the lighthouse beam,
A broken spar, breaks its pulse.

"What have I learned of word or line?"
Ticks on, ticks off; ticks on, ticks off.
The bay, that was a clotted eye,
Is turned to water by the dark.
Only my summer breaks upon
The sea, the gulls, the narrow land.

THE HEART

In the midst of words your wordless image
Marches through the precincts of my night
And all the structures of my language lie undone:
The bright cathedrals clatter, and the moon-
Topped spires break their stalk.
Sprawled-before that raid, I watch the towns

Go under. And in the waiting dark, I loose
Like marbles spinning from a child
The crazed and hooded creatures of the heart.

AROUND ONE CELLINI SALTCELLAR

Neptune, his trident, and horses of gold,
Breaks the blue, enameled waves,
Blue for the sea, whose salt
He holds towards Tellus
On the coral shore. She,
Bright goddess, nudely gold.

Salt within the running blood
Is all our relic of the sea,
Diamonded and jeweled as these
Bright coruscations of a crown.
Salt within the running tear
Can taste of pagan artifice.

Intricate and wrought as this,
Mortality's an excellence;
The sea surge hobbled by
The gold hand of the artisan;
The blood, drying of its salt
For Neptune, as he lounges there.

THE EYE, THE PULSE

The air extends beyond this sill
And, whether I will or not, performs
Its various delights. So children
Race upon the sand and cry
Their colorful syllables, gulls

In rocky congregations cry.
All one mesh and all one dance
Upon the inner ear and eye.

The air extends, and through its light
The mind in intellection moves,
Conning the landscape to a line
Of liquid spars and sanded flats.

The body in projection moves
Into the threaded air and sky.
And now begins the true delight.
The sympathy of life for life
Leaps past formal excellence.
Eros, bringer of delight,
Quickens the landscape to a pulse.
Sand, and child, and formal bird
Stand at the center of our love,
As at the center of this globe
The jewel-spun open and shut
Of an insect's breathing.

ON A LINE BY LAWRENCE

There is no violence the eye can't tame.
Fire dances through the scribbled ant.
The perfect rose is only a running flame.

Who looks for comfort has himself to blame
If he sicken at all the reddish rant.
There is no violence the eye can't tame.

Man's stable mathematic cannot maim
This energy that catches it aslant.
The perfect rose is only a running flame.

I see your nakedness, and for it claim
The flare, the synergy that will not scant.
There is no violence the eye can't tame.

The world runs riot underneath its frame.
Though many poets sweeten to enchant,
The perfect rose is only a running flame.

Man in his divinity became
The fire that has all fire for his grant.
There is no violence the eye can't tame.
The perfect rose is only a running flame.

SUMMER

A slow net of stars drags the bay.
The air shining night and day
Of a perpetual splendor.
So earth rarefies to water,
Water to air, air to fire.

Flared out of heaven,
The sea dropping there,
That corona toward which the sight is pulled.
And here, in the very inch of summer
Where sensation is compressed to charge,
Fire finds the air,
Of a splendor perpetual.

You in your element,
Knot of elements,
Somewhere between shore, and sea, and sky
Turn face to the dark,
Waiting that full stop, the shock, the run
Of flesh to fire,
The rare, the awful visitor.
Voice, the perch of speech, finding dominion.

DECEMBER

White as aspirin the white snow
Lies banked along the veins.
It chills desire to sorrow.

All day we stayed within our rooms
And tapped the sound of summer,
The bee's sound that was a place
Of isolation. Easily, in tides,
The whiteness washes us again
As sun's unseasonal projection.

In dark apartments glitter
Of talk, of moving forms,
Is distant. Snow falls
Upon the sin of our involvement.

ANOTHER OLD SONG

The swans upon their lake of glass
And all that symbolist furniture
Begin to fade. My hand raps hard.
That rapping hard reduces to
The frail tapping of a pencil
Upon glass, where nothing chimes.

Each day must seek its music out
Else that frozen continent
Will turn to us the blind stare,
Not to be moved by stars or gulls.
Conscripted to the dark surface
Of the night, the eye expires.

But this verse and I contrive a machine
To rattle my scattered souvenirs:
I see that furious summer come
Where I stood helpless on the shore;
Bewitched by water, spidery stars,
I see another old song start.

If you whom I recall exist
Within this frozen pulse, ticking
In the dark, if you exist
In any form of fire, come close.
(Feed this, equally false,
To the swans upon their lake of glass.)

ENTERS LIGHT

Though I see earth clean
As in the first philosophies,
Formed of a single substance,
Be it fire or air,

This spirit wavering,
Dark fluxion, all
Unfixable by thought,
Is the "I" seeing;

And shall be, until light,
The dramatic person, enters in
To his inheritance.

Until then, as after then,
May the center live
In his circumference.

POWER IN AMERICA

The struck animal, blurred
By subsequent hours, lies
Upon the road, hunched fur and spirit.
At night, drawn by the hum of power,
Then doubled into pain, sight smashed,
It caught the radicals of
Descending speed, their brilliance.

Or the boy in Dreiser's novel,
That blind head, felled
By the big city hotel,
Its monolithic shine and scramble.
Even Crane, who tried to make
A shining steel structure of a bridge
Lead him out, caught by the brilliance
That kills, in America.

As at the movie's close,
Man alone, against the wall,
Watches the lights move in,
The fugitive, hatless there,
And we, thrilled into our fear,
See the enormously wheeled clatter,
Glistening, never in error,
Rise to break his back.

DEATH OF A GRANDMOTHER

Let me borrow her corpse a little.
Over that clown in finest linen,
Over that white-dressed dummy, pretty girl,
(Dressed for a party, the daughters cried)
Let me speak a line.

The dead lie in a ditch of fear,
In an earth wound, in an old mouth
That has sucked them there.
My grandmother drank tea, and wailed
As if the Wailing Wall kissed her head
Beside the kitchen window;
While the flaking, green-boxed radio
Retailed in Yiddish song
And heartache all day long.
Or laughter found her,
The sly, sexual humor of the grave.

Yet after her years of dragging leg,
Of yellowed sight,
She still found pain enough
To polish off the final hours with a shriek.
To what sweet kingdom do the old Jews go?
Now mourned by her radio and bed,
She wishes me health and children,
Who am her inheritor.

I sing her a song of praise.
She meddled with my childhood
Like a witch, and I can meet her
Curse for curse in that slum heaven where we go
When this American dream is spent—
To give her a crust of bread, a little love.

FROM

Mountain, Fire, Thornbush

1961

THE DESTRUCTIVE WILL

This, then, is the child's wish:
To see the earth a dancing flood
And the new home floating free,
And all irrational, outside, inside.
The packed beasts padding through
The comforts of the living room.
And the old man, his hand forced
By the impossible command,
Compass lost and out of touch.
And all the navigational aids
Part of the swiftly moving flood.
But mainly it's the murderous beasts,
Wonderfully close and now accepted
As part of home and family:
The dumb, the fierce, the tooth and claw.
I read it in the earliest book,
Where all our childhoods signify
Themselves in open imagery.
And this is the image of the will:
To see the globe a watery blot,
History killed, pain stopped.
And this must win us to the dark,
And close our eyes, and rock our sleep,
And pray the coffin be an ark.

THE PROPHET ANNOUNCES

on an illustration from an eighteenth-century Haggadah

And so they arrive for all the world to see,
Elijah with the shofar to his mouth,
His hand upon the guide reins of the King,
Who rides an ass. They look so sad.
In all, a quiet scene, unless the shofar's sound
I barely hear was louder in that century.
Behind them is a tree, and on its branch
A startled bird, to say there's hope of life.

Old images of immortality.
But where's new Adam come to greet the King?
Unless this be the moment of their setting out,
And no one's heard that death's been done and even
Now the first light's traveling from the east.

LINES FOR THE ANCIENT SCRIBES

The past sends images to beach
Upon our present consciousness.
The sons of light war with the sons
Of darkness still. The congregations
Of the sleek and sure rule at will.

Jerome and Origen can tell
How Greek redactions of the text
Stalled at the Tetragrammaton.
And violent in archaic script
The Name burned upon parchment—

Whence springs the ram to mind again
From whose sinews David took
Ten strings to fan upon his harp.
So that the sacrifice was song,
Though ash lay on the altar stone.

ADORATION OF THE MOON

for Max Weber

Sappho's moist lotus and the scudding moon
Speak to each other in a dilation upon Acheron.
Lean out of the abyss of origin four ragged Jews,
Masters of wrath and judgment, gentled by the moon.
Their tall hats rise, their faces lengthen
As o the spell is on them. Three grip
The word for ballast, while the fourth,

Beard upended, sniffs the moon-fleck as it falls.
Support them in flight, goddess,
That when the darkness comes, thy light put out,
Their candle's flame send up in steep aroma
The scholar's must.

THE TALKER

from a Midrash

While all the choiring angels cried:
Creation's crown is set awry!
God fabled man before he was,
And boasting of His enterprise
Bade angels say the simple names
That mark in place each bird and beast.

But they were dumb, as He foretold—
When man stepped from the shuddering dust
And lightly tossed the syllables,
And said his own name, quick as dirt.
Then angels crept into their spheres,
And dirt, and bird, and beast were his.

THE MARRIAGE

When they were canopied, and had the wine
To lace their spirits in the trembling cup,
And all the holy words sang round their heads
In tribute to the maker and the vine,
He saw the leeching sea lap, like darkness,
Up her summer's gown, as if dark time
And he should race to claim the maidenhead.
When he smashed the cup, then ruin spread.
The dazzled floor showed sea and blood.
Beyond this harvest that the ritual bore
(Their mothers weeping on the farther shore)

From *Mountain, Fire, Thornbush*, 1961 ✤ 37

They saw the journeying years extend.
And Zion's hill rose for their reckoning.

THE BOOK

Violent in its blood, the dark book
Hangs like a tree of night upon the sky.
It batters history, that genesis,
Word that whelped a world up,
While priest and king and all
Raged at the syntax they were swaddled by.

And this is law, or so is said
Within the darkening synagogue
By old men, honored in their beards
By the unsealed, heroic sounds.
Celebration without end, the dark book
Whispers to the wind,
Wind cradles the destructive globe.

Outside, the night is far away.
Space is empty. One might touch,
If the necessary power were given,
All with human eloquence.
What hangs upon the tree is man.
With his blood the book is written.

EXODUS

When they escaped
They carried a pack of bones
In a mummy-coffin like an ark.
Of course they had the pillar
Of clouds by day and fire by night,
But those were like dreams
Or something painted on the sky.

God was in the bones
Because Joseph had said,
God will remember you
If you take me hence.
This was before the miracle
By the sea or the thundering mountain,
Before the time of thrones
And cherubim. They were
Only now drawn forth
To eat the history feast
And begin the journey.
Why then should they carry history
Like an ark, and the remembering
Already begun?

PHAROS

On the High Priest's tunic
Golden pomegranates, silver bells.
Alexander, off for Egypt,
Was stilled by the luster of robes.
Bright as that boy-god's city
When it stood
Second town to Rome,
The Priest's robe must have gathered
Such light as Pharos throws.
On the day of festival
They sailed to the Island—
Jews and many others—
"Reverencing the place in which
The light of interpretation
First shone forth."
A god was translated
By those rabbis.
The sibylline oracles
Spoke Messianic prophecies.
The gates of allegory
Are never closed.

ALEPH

Oxhead, working in
The intelligence. First sign,
Alphabet's wedge.
Followed by house, fish,
Man praying, palm of hand,
Water, serpent,
Eye, and so forth—cross.
Whence to
Hebrew-Phoenician abstract
And so to Greek.
But to return to first
Signs when the world's
Complex—
The head of an ox
Blunt, blundering,
Withal intelligencer
Pushing forward, horns raised,
Stirring the matter
To make a beginning
For Amos, Homer,
And all who came first
In that sign.

THE ROUGH PROOF

These are the eminent journeyers:
Father, and son, and serving men,
The saddled ass and the gathered wood.
Across the morning, like polished stone
Hangs the three-day-distant hill.

In the dark thicket, on the mount,
Innocence, the tangled ram,
Waits for the metaphor to kill.
It is earliest time. Light
Travels the knife, as it did the will.

ANOTHER READING

What if the ancient had dreamed it,
If there had been no calling,
Only the need that makes each one
Sacrifice to have his gift again
Spoke in him, and brute, blind,
He pushed his son to the rim of that need,
Before God touched terror down
And the manic wish ran free?

A SHORT HISTORY

Urbanity obscures the mystery.
From the fiery limits of His crown
The brawling letters broke,
In the beginning.
Violence on the historical track.
Then distances—prophet, king—
and the voltage that enabled them
To strike their meaning
And to stand. When the palmed word
Issued anodyne. The rest is mockery.

MOUNTAIN, FIRE, THORNBUSH

How everything gets tamed.
The pronominal outcry, as if uttered in ecstasy,
Is turned to syntax. We are
Only a step from discursive prose
When the voice speaks from the thornbush.
Mountain, fire, and thornbush.
Supplied only with these, even that aniconic Jew
Could spell mystery. But there must be
Narrative. The people must get to the mountain.
Doors must open and close.

How to savor the savagery of Egyptians,
Who betrayed the names of their gods
To demons, and tore the hair
From their godheads
As lotus blossoms are pulled out of the pool.

FEAST OF THE RAM'S HORN

As seventh sign, the antique heavens show
A pair of scales. And Jews, no less antique,
Hear the ram-rod summons beat their heels,
Until they stand together in mock show
As if they meant to recognize a king.

For they are come again to this good turning:
That from the mountain where their leader goes,
In ten days' time they greet the Law descending.
And these are ancient stories from a book
That circulates, and for them has no ending.

All stand as witness to the great event.
Ezra, their scribe, before the water gate
Takes up the book, and the people rise.
And those who weep upon the word are bid
To hold their peace because the day is holy.

Feast of the ram's horn. Let the player rise.
And may the sound of that bent instrument,
In the seventh month, before the seventh gate,
Speak for all the living and the dead,
And tell creation it is memorized.

Let Isaac be remembered in the ram
That when the great horn sounds, and all are come,
These who now are gathered as one man
Shall be gathered again. Set the bright
Scales in the sky until that judgment's done.

FROM A SERMON ON THE FIVE AFFLICTIONS

Soul, the wanderer, fetch it out
And make it sing in holiness
And hop in God's hand all the day
And preen itself in loveliness.
Five afflictions are the way.

Because the soul is living wick
And flames in its vitality,
Deny yourself both food and drink.
Imitate mortality.
Soul will shake itself and flee.

Because the soul is unity,
Within the coupling dark lie still.
Let body in its agony
Cry to have itself fulfilled.
Soul will know itself unwilled.

The soul is spirit, and spirit shines
As pennies do in a cupped hand.
But the hand, if washed, can shine so too.
Keep precious water from your skin
And spirit will not stay within.

The soul is an unchanging thing.
It cannot weight itself with grit.
But body, when anointed,
Puts on a like purity.
Slime yourself, and soul will flee.

Soul, like wind, is lifted up,
Like waves, and like the sea spray.
Let a man go barefoot, and he must
In his heaviness draw dust.
And soul, unhoused, is on its way.

Soul, the wanderer, fetch it out
And make it sing in holiness
And hop in God's hand all the day
And preen itself in loveliness.
Five afflictions are the way.

SPIRIT OF RABBI NACHMAN

"The word moves a bit of air,
And this the next, until it reaches
The man who receives the word of his friend
And receives his soul therein
And is therein awakened"—
Rabbi Nachman's preachment on the word,
Which I gloomily thumb
Wondering how it is with me
That I am not yet on the first
Rung (and many with me!)
To move a bit of air!

If a man ask, can he have
This thing, whether it be
An infusion of soul, or souls,
Steadfast to complete the journeying?
Words moving a bit of air
So that the whole morning moves.

Battle Report

1966

NEWS OF THE WORLD

The past, like so many bad poems,
Waits to be reordered,
And the future needs reordering too.
Rain dampens the brick,
And the house sends up its smell
Of smoke and lives—
My own funk the major part.
Angling for direction,
I think of the favored in Homer,
Who in a dream, a council meeting,
At the bottom of despair,
Heard the voice of a god or goddess,
Though it was, say, only Polites
Speaking. Turning to a friend,
I ask again
For news of the world.

MONDAY

Everybody thinks the past is real.
The window and the skull
Admit light. The past comes through
Like that—undifferentiated,
Hallucinatory, of no weight.
Sleepless that night, he saw the
Room close-woven, a nest
Of chairs, tables, rug
The past was filtering through.
It had no odor, no
Emotion. You could not
Say that in the silences
The past came in
Like water over sand.
There was no movement.
You could not draw the blind.

RITES

And the Collectors make the rounds
Continually. What a perpetual payment
Of old fingernails, hair, skin parings:
The detritus of life, not to be grudged.
But what else they take from me
Minute by minute—heart's ease,
Zeal of success . . .
Should I be judged,
Can I demand payment for this life
That they take from me continually?

THE COLLECTORS

I can sit here, in the quietness,
With nothing but the refrigerator hum
To spell mortality, and imagine
The Collectors come for the sagging brain,
Lugged flesh, tired lungs.
"Right here, men!" I shout,
In that manner I lacked
All my life.

SUNDAY MORNING

You begin to tell a story.
I perceive it is to be
Another of those unpunctuated excursions
Into the country of my failures.
You, pointing to the familiar landmarks.
I, nodding in assent.
We settle back.

PAST TIME

I believe we came together
Out of ignorance, not love,
Both being shy and hunted in the city.
In the hot summer, touching each other,
Amazed at how love could come
Like a waterfall, with frightening force
And bruising sleep. Waking at noon,
Touching each other for direction,
Out of ignorance, not love.

HOW MANY TIMES

How many times
Can you go back to the same scene
With love? I never hope to know.
We work patiently at our quarrels,
Starting them now like love,
Deliberately but with elaborate
Ease. When they catch
We marvel at the blaze,
Crowding in close.
"Inexhaustible." We shout at one another,
Happy for the moment.
I never hope to know
How many times.

THE INJUNCTION

He went about freeing imaginary birds,
Making gestures like freeing them;
The birds were imaginary
But the gestures were real.
Spirit is real even when it rides
And hides in sick motions of the body,

Where I spy it daily
And repeat to myself
The injunction:
Choose life.

THREE DAYS

On Wednesday he chose life
And went about getting breakfast
With a light heart. He looked at people,
Considered plants and stones,
Wrote letters to distant friends.
At nightfall he was back in the slough,
Hip-deep, and the stuff
Pulling him under. So he asked himself,
How is it life obviously
Does not choose you?
And what does your choice come to then?
Thursday he had no answer
And the sick spirit withered.
Friday he dropped the metaphor.

HIS LIFE

When he writes about his life
He just rakes it back
And forth. It's still
His life, so he rakes it.

FORCES

He was given over to forces that made him idle.
They came about him, rubbing their fur.
Rank with it, they stayed against his trembling,

His dizziness, his crying out
For an end to the shifting and blurring,
To the wanderings
That will not yet reveal themselves.

FOR JOB AT FORTY

Who would have thought you'd get this far,
Fingering the spots where the boils will be,
Your prosperity before you?
What a picture of absent plagues,
Dunghills, encrusted sores.
What a mark for the spoiler,
Who is there, at the corner,
And now you turn his way.

WHAT THE WITCH SAID

I would not want to see
Gods ascending out of the earth
Or the dead living.
How can they talk so easily
Of a stone rolled
From the cave's mouth,
Of spirits crowding a ditch to drink?
What banquet
Draws them to the dead,
What tender eating?

THE SERVICE

Where the wash of the world
Filled me with the brine of
Dead things, gone things.

From *Battle Report*, 1966   ❖   51

To wake to the illusion
Of meaning, more than
The illusion of beauty,
I have come back to
The lion and lioness,
Facing each other,
The two sides of the cloth,
To read the service again.
In my breath, the halted,
The stunned, the shattered without
Movement. Lion and lioness
Do what they will.

DECISIONS

The night was moving to another decision
I would hear about later
And not recognize. "I am
The bitter name," said Death.
"Surely, you believe in me."

To taste in the lees of sleep.

THESE LIVES

When everything is prepared for the feast—
August high-vaulted,
The clouds a classic scroll—
The painter must have a hypo.
What's the meaning of his crying jag?
The wife calls the doctor.

The dolphin floats gently to shore
On the winds of his own corruption.
Even the gulls respect that stench.

What happens to these lives?

BEYOND THE DEMONIC ELEMENT

I cast out
Beyond the demonic element
And the fear of death
(And the fear of death)
Into that bright water
Beyond this water
Where leviathan swims.
Communication is instant
When it comes—close
As my hand, the words on my tongue,
Though the crying in my ear
Is my own death crying.

A WRITER

That one wrote out of a life lived,
So I envied him. Naturally,
I could imitate his manner.
But the life lived (which, believe me,
I do not want to hear about)
Was his. To others I leave
The memory of themselves.

CAPTAIN

"Old solitary whiff-beard,"
As another poet has sung you,
I pass you twice a day
Corner of Fulton and Cranberry—
Palms up, pushing the spirit—
On my way toward work or wife,
To the subway or returning.
And you were after?
"A Passage to India,"
Mottoes the bronze plaque
On the brick of the Spanish eatery
Where your leaves were first collected.
Though I remember
"Come lovely and soothing death"
Where I wound it into my skull—
A depressed kid of twelve—
As tight as the mockingbird's shuttle,
I never take up your book.
Serenely arriving, arriving,
You coast to each young poet.
Your day, delicate death,
And Century!

FOR DAVID

Someone is writing
"Illuminator of the Paths,"
Or has already
Written it, though
I cannot find it
On my shelf,
Or is even now
Walking his room
With the book
In his head.

ABC OF CULTURE

So the angel of death whistles Mozart
(As we knew he would)
Bicycling amid the smoke of Auschwitz,
The Jews of Auschwitz,
In the great museum of Western Art.

THE NIGHT

Memory, my own prince of disaster,
My ancient of night.
In the scored silence
I see the dead.
They file past the fixed camera—
The ritual wave, and the smile,
And goodnight. For an instant
They are there, caught
In their clothes and their gestures;
Their white faces glow
In the murk of the film,
Absurdly alive. How little I own
This family of the dead,
Who are now part of night.
Memory, my own prince of disaster,
When you go,
Where's the night?

THEY

Strength cannot be resurrected
Unless it has slept in secrecy.
In the husks of forgetting
The power of memory grows.
On the day of destruction

Power lies at the bottom.
They sit on the ground.
They visit graves.

DUMB ADAM

I forget. Was it to be
Letters of black fire on white fire
Or letters of white fire on black fire?
But here are the words.
The vines of heart-shaped leaves
Bind the trees
Yet the topmost branches remain free
To receive signals.

The freedom to glide, to coast.
The car rolling without gas,
The gull shifting from
Current to current with stationary
Wings. The clouds swing west
For another easy victory.
It is a sickness that hollows
Your life and your words.

Dumb Adam, slow-footed,
You are like the farmers
I pass in their fields;
Your world has vanished.
It is all the wind and water
Of before creation.

Along the night routes,
In the brightness of cities,
I read letters of black fire
On white fire.

MASTER AND TEACHER

Teach me the only beginning.
Point me to the god
Of the hidden time.
When I say the old names
Of mountains and rivers,
Put the map in my hand.

THE SIX HUNDRED THOUSAND LETTERS

The day like blank paper
Being pulled from my typewriter.
With the six
Hundred thousand letters of the Law
Surrounding me,
Not one of them in place.

PURITIES

What was ceremonially impure, he knew,
Was his life. The laws were not followed.
The god was unhonored.
Anxiety sat on every road.
To change his life, he invented
A job that promised regularity and order.
He invented love that promised joy.
In summer he sat among green trees.
The family laughed in water.
Now let the ceremony begin, he said,
In the heart of summer,
In the pure green
And the pure blue.
Let the god walk his mountain.
He can come down.

From *Battle Report*, 1966   ⚜   57

HIDDEN

My own breath
is hidden in the universe.
Why should I concern myself?
It rises and falls
With all the others,
So that I find it
Easy to begin.

THE OLD NOSTALGIA

"The Night the Old Nostalgia
Burned Down" is
The most beautiful
Title in American writing.
Every night I visit it—
Crammed full of heroes,
Blondes, girls out of
My own childhood and the neighborhood.
Tenderly I light the flesh
And watch it go, like dreams:
Mother and father burning down
To the sweet music
Of Stephen Foster, hymned
In the P.S. 3 assembly.
Every day is a new beginning,
The charred remains
Softening the scent of bleak
December; background music
Against which criss-cross
Rapid images of a new life.
I leave the scene
Confident the spectacle
Has enduring worth,
Will light me a long way,
Songs to sing.

NATIONAL COLD STORAGE COMPANY

The National Cold Storage Company contains
More things than you can dream of.
Hard by the Brooklyn Bridge it stands
In a litter of freight cars,
Tugs to one side; the other, the traffic
Of the Long Island Expressway.
I myself have dropped into it in seven years
Midnight tossings, plans for escape, the shakes.
Add this to the national total—
Grant's tomb, the Civil War, Arlington,
The young President dead.
Above the warehouse and beneath the stars
The poets creep on the harp of the Bridge.
But see,
They fall into the National Cold Storage Company
One by one. The wind off the river is too cold,
Or the times too rough, or the Bridge
Is not a harp at all. Or maybe
A monstrous birth inside the warehouse
Must be fed by everything—ships, poems,
Stars, all the years of our lives.

BATTLE REPORT

I
The Adriatic was no sailor's sea.
We raced above that water for our lives
Hoping the green curve of Italy
Would take us in. Rank, meaningless fire

That had no other object but our life
Raged in the stunned engine. I acquired
From the scene that flickered like a silent film
New perspective on the days of man.

Now the aviators, primed for flight,
Gave to the blue expanse can after can
Of calibers, armored clothes, all
The rich paraphernalia of our war.

Death in a hungry instant took us in.
He touched me where my lifeblood danced
And said, the cold water is an ample grin
For all your twenty years.

Monotone and flawless, the blue sky
Shows to my watching face this afternoon
The chilled signal of our victory.
Again the lost plane drums home.

2
No violence rode in the glistening chamber.
For the gunner the world was unhinged.
Abstract as a drinker and single
He hunched to his task, the dumb show
Of surgical fighters, while flak, impersonal,
Beat at the floor that he stood on.

The diamond in his eye was fear;
It barely flickered.
From target to target he rode.
The images froze, the flak hardly mattered.
Europe rolled to its murderous knees
Under the sex of guns and cannon.

In an absence of pain he continued,
The oxygen misting his veins like summer.
The bomber's long sleep and the cry of the gunner,
Who knows that the unseen mime in his blood
Will startle to terror,
Years later, when love matters.

3
My pilot dreamed of death before he died.
That stumbling Texas boy
Grew cold before the end, and told
The bombardier, who told us all.
We worried while we slept.
And when he died, on that dark morning
Over Italy in clouds,
We clapped him into dirt.
We counted it for enmity
That he had fraternized with death.
From hand to hand
We passed in wonderment
The quicksilver of our lives.

4
I turn my rubber face to the blue square
Given me to trace the fighters
As they weave their frost, and see
Within this sky the traffic
Fierce and heavy for the day:
All those who stumbling home at dark
Found their names fixed
Beside a numbered Fort, and heard
At dawn the sirens rattling the night away,
And rose to that cold resurrection
And are now gathered over Italy.

In this slow dream's rehearsal,
Again I am the death-instructed kid,
Gun in its cradle, sun at my back,
Cities below me without sound.
That tensed, corrugated hose
Feeding to my face the air of substance,
I face the mirroring past.
We swarm the skies, determined armies,
To seek the war's end, the silence stealing,
The mind grown hesitant as breath.

FROM

This World

1971

FOR WCW

Now they are trying to make you
The genital thug, leader
Of the new black shirts—
Masculinity over all!
I remember you after the stroke
(Which stroke? I don't remember which stroke.)
Afraid to be left by Flossie
In a hotel lobby, crying out
To her not to leave you
For a minute. Cracked open
And nothing but womanish milk
In the hole. Only a year
Before that we were banging
On the door for a girl to open,
To both of us. Cracked,
Broken. Fear
Slaughtering the brightness
Of your face, stroke and
Counterstroke, repeated and
Repeated, for anyone to see.
And now, grandmotherly,
You stare from the cover
Of your selected poems—
The only face you could compose
In the end. As if having
Written of love better than any poet
Of our time, you stepped over
To that side for peace.
What valleys, William, to retrace
In memory, after the masculine mountains,
What long and splendid valleys.

DAYS AND NIGHTS

1

You keep beating me down.
When I reach a balance,
You break it, always
Clawing for the heart.
In the electric light
We face each other.
Whatever you want of me,
Goddess of insomnia and pure form,
It's not these messages I scratch out
Morning after morning
To turn you off.

2

Whether I had room
For all that joy
In my economy
Is another matter.
Rejecting me,
She shut out all my light,
Showed to me the backs
Of houses, tail lights
Going fast,
Smiles disappearing.
Every man
Was my enemy.
So it was for many a day.
I could not
Climb out of it,
So close was I
To her will.

3

"He that is wise may correct natures."
Alchemy. The philosophical stone.
Your shadow over the page.
Your hair to my cheek.
Your eyes great riding lights

In the alcoholic storm that now
I remember, along with that
Bruising sweat of rhetoric
I thought appropriate to the times.
He that is wise
May have his life to remember.
But I am reduced to reciting
The letters of the alphabet.
If I say them with fervor
(Saying them with fervor)
Will memory be stirred?
Your own goddess-voice
In the leaves, in the night
Of the body, as I turn the page.

4
Well, it was only Bottom's dream—
Methought I was and
Methought I had.
Outside, the sky is a field
In which the seeds of minerals shine.
And I am hunched over the board
On which I write my nights
Breathing configurations
On the winter air. As far from you
As ever I was far from you.
The cold locks everything in place.
Now I am here. The flame of my match
Everything that is given to me.

5
Suddenly I see your face close up
And all my senses scramble
To get the shock
Home again. In sleep
Not knowing who I am
Or however that spent match struck.

6

The white brilliance under the eyelids
So that all things appear to me
In that color. The worlds you see
Exist in joy. Eyes like doves.
Equilibrium, a white brilliance.

7

Now you come again
Like a very patient ghost,
Offering me Zen records,
A discourse on the stomach
As the seat of the soul,
Your long white neck to kiss.
The tiger's eye that is
Your favorite jewel
Shines in your hand.
Wanting to, I can't conjure
You up, not a touch.
Unbidden, you cross a thousand miles
To say, This is the gift
I was going to give you forever.

THE LESSON

While other cases
Lean away from the nominative,
The poet is giving the girl
Large roses.
They are blood-red roses.
They require no prepositions
As they come through
To the girl, become
The girl's face and body;
And wholly blood-red
Are fixed in the nominative
Like a pulse.

THE LIGHT IS SOWN

The light is sown.
It is there, under the stones
That have been flung
On the street.
Behind my house now
It is in full flower.
The leaves of the mimosa
Are edged with light.
This is the gift
I have and do not claim.
If I could take
The world like that—
All things to which
The light adheres:
Your body edged with light
Which I claim
And count on
And lose
And claim again.

BY THE WOMEN'S HOUSE OF DETENTION

Love is the beggar's itch
And I depart
Past the stockaded women, tier on tier,
Singing the same song
Through their delicate home.

Sundays, the colored lesbians
Lean in the street and cry
Up to the latticed windows
Love's old sweet song.

Happy in these streets
I see out of some dark cellar
Orpheus lead Eurydice

While past me goes
Young Icarus, his red heart
Bleating like a sheep
In the fall from perpetual music.

This summer, like a jungle,
I dream in a confusion of chairs
As love over the ancient city
Flares like an angel's eye.

GLORY

In the museum of antiquities
I ran my hands over
The breasts and thighs
Of the young Aphrodite
And heard her say, kiss my ass.

RECAPITULATIONS

1
Those were not salt tears.
My mouth in your hand
Appeared to be drinking.
The words were lost.
A drunken sleep.
Only your turning to your name
As I desperately say.

2
I was wearing those funny socks,
Businessmen's hose,
And dreaming you loved me.
I was strung so tight

And the socks were so free
In your jeans, and your hair,
And your twenty-one years.

3
Tell me I have the right
To live among these images.
High up on the building wall
A niche for the image. For you
Pan and the nymphs,
The inscription in Greek
On that one. Stunned
By their sun and silence
I step carefully through traffic
So as not to disturb the smile
Where you have turned to stone.

4
Rain this night
Falls on the past.
That hard ground
Doesn't catch a drop.

MINUTE BIOGRAPHY

He thought of himself
As in the service of a lady
Or of the moon.
Though in truth
He was in the service
Of a style that was
Trying to grow
Hands and feet
And so had need of him
And filled his life.

AMERICAN WORDS

The kids outside are breaking bottles
Because they have bottles in their hands.
Thinking of marriage
Because the words have a target.
After dark the traffic
Makes a kind of undersong.
I close my eyes
And watch the nighttime ferries
Like lighted keyboards.
What they play upon
Stretches like romance,
Night, an American life.

DEAR WIFE

Your tears will silk the pillow
And raise a luxury of weeds.
When those weeds find my headstone
We are both at peace.

AS I COME HOME

The players cry
"Reason" in Hamlet
And it is a ghost.
My own face
Shuffles at the windowpane.
Whatever I look through
Is deception—clear as that
Ghostly player crying
"Reason" when I hear "Revenge."
And murder is loose
On the broad highway.
My family digging for

Shelter as I come home,
Saying,
I give you this gift
Of reason.

FIRST SNOW

The first snow of winter
And in my early morning dream
You with one breast uncovered
Talk to me
Of the possibilities of life.

The cats don't know what to do.
They roam the house.
We're all trying
To perceive where
Our happiness lies.

Through the shutters and closed windows
I hear the crunch of tires.
Nothing in my life
Is as clear to me.

Silence
Like snow.
At forty-four
To be back
In the drifts!

FACING A WALL

1
I take up my position:
To make sense of that wall.

2
When they say
History doesn't matter,
Do they mean lives?

3
Among these many voices,
The voice of a friend,
On the level.

4
Glacial.
Nothing moves
But the ice.

5
You are too dependent
On what is placed before you:
The sea, a sunset,
A long life.

6
Without difficulty,
To bring words
Into this world.

7
In a country of trees
Prepare the way for the desert.

WORKING IT OUT

1
What is it that I have to do?
My body accuses me,
The cause of its uselessness.
My imagination
Turns its pockets inside out.

I explain everything
At length
And set it down.
My need, I cry,
My need. But you
Walk away from it
As if to say
Ah, you're only trying
To change your life.

2

I watch my life hour by hour.
I call it a natural process,
Even organic growth.
Hidden in its proliferating
Activities, mortgages, lusts
There is a mind
Probably tracing a shape.
In moments of stress
That mind seems to be watching me,
Anxious for a response.
Then I nod to show
I am satisfied with the arrangement
If it is.

3
We're all attached to our lives.
Some strongly, some
By the thinnest of lines.
But at times
We seem to be floating
Or our lives floating
One from the other
In a great happiness.

SISTER

My dead sister dreams away her life.
About forty years of dreaming
As I count.
My father blamed my mother
For the child's death
And wasn't at the funeral.
The tears, the tears she bred
In me out of my sister's loss,
Weeping of hurt, deprivation, age,
The insanity of life.
My sister, eager for her share,
Under such a tiny headstone
In a city we never pass.
Kin, dreaming dark poems
That spill into my life.

TO MY FATHER

Whatever it was
Illuminating me
With dreams

I saw your face
Words on your eyelids

Windows on all four sides
To let the light in

What would you do
With this body
You would die in it
Again

You would not even
Write these poems.

SPACES

1

Quickening his step, my father
Came into the room.
Now I will tell you about myself,
He said.
When I write these words
A torpor comes over me.
I can hardly hold the pen.

2

If you want to become a wall,
Work at it. More plaster, I mean,
And more paint.
Get the job done.

3

To be summoned like that
Startles me.
I put on the light
At 2 A.M.
And stand
At the edge of a field.

4

Putting words
To these sounds
You have your own
Victory.
But to recognize it.

TO THE TEACHER

1

That the galaxy is a river of light
That the order of seeds is in my hand
I ask to enter this world without confusion.

2

The enormous lights
And mysteries of this world
Which the teacher says
I shut from myself
With a hand,
Spending my sight
On these snarled lines,
This closed-in town
Where I walk and work
And find you in sleep
In the dark room, the dark town,
In a life that I cannot
Honestly call the way.

3

He has been asking for help
Everywhere for his child
With the clogged tongue.
Not that the boy
Should speak with eloquence.
But that he should speak
His need—to the world,
The citizens. The barest
Speech. I am happy.
I am sad.
The sense is beautiful.

4

The reader begins
With the destruction of the city.
It is the same tune
Every day for a week now.
But how he appears to enjoy
That rattle of words.
Crowds fleeing, others
Looting shops
In the most expensive
Avenues of the city.
Smoke like a cowl

Over the words
And the reader's body.
He must experience it
To the end
Each day, as it was set down
From the roots of heaven.

5
In the sequence
The angel of each verse
Stands like a point of flame.

FROM MARTIN BUBER

"A story must be told in such a way
That it constitutes help in itself."
Or not the way telephone addicts
Trap themselves for eternity
In a recital of symptoms—
Blood pressure, urine, sleep—
Saying tonight what they will
Relive tomorrow.

(Finding you whole
After a night of hatred
World to my touch
Like bread to my touch
Which I ceaselessly crumble
And the loaf is there.)

(Or when the traffic slurs
Early in the morning
Of a long night
And I strike it rich
With calm.)

THE SYNAGOGUE ON KANE STREET

Anachronisms are pleasant.
I like shifting periods
As the young rabbi doesn't shift tones
Saying "The Ethics of Maimonides"
And "The Reader's Digest."

There is no reason for survival.
As we drift outward
The tribal gods wave farewell.

It is the mother synagogue of Brooklyn.
We are a handful in a cathedral.

When I was asked
I said the blessing
For the reading of the scroll
Almost correctly.

The reader had a silver pointer.

The parchment before me
Was like a beginning.

RIVERSIDE DRIVE

from the Yiddish of Joseph Rolnick

Pulling myself out of bed,
I leave the house.
The blueness caresses me.
The wind pushes my hair.
A whole world of quiet
I fill with my steps
On the sidewalk,
And in the street,
The milkman's horse.
Somewhere, on a higher floor,

Along a dark corridor,
The milkman makes his shining rows.
Running, the papers
Under my arm,
I don't look at numbers.
I know the way
Like the horse.
The sun is already up
On the east side of the city.
Its flames, its grace
Spill, whole canfuls, on the cliffs
Of the Jersey shore.
At 310 Riverside Drive
A man on a low balcony,
Young but with mustache and beard—
His appearance not of here—
Stretches a hand toward
The west and shouts
Something like, See there!
And I stand like him
With my papers raised
Like an offering
To the light.
The two of us
Come for the first time
To this place,
To the red cliffs
Of this morning.

DITTY

Where did the Jewish god go?
Up the chimney flues.
Who saw him go?
Six million souls.
How did he go?
All so still
As dew from the grass.

THE WAY

Why are you crying in Israel,
Brother, I ask as I switch over
To the emergency oxygen.
Do we have to dig up all
The Freudian plumbing
To reconstruct our lives?
If I had clean air like you,
I think I could breathe.
As it is my mouthpiece keeps
Clogging and my eyes blur.
I can barely make it
Between the desks.
And you, walking
Between orange trees
Among the companions,
And still so far from the way.

WHERE I AM NOW

Every morning I look
Into the world
And there is no renewal.
Every night, my lids clamped,
I concentrate
On the renewal to come.
I am on the lookout for
A great illumining,
Prepared to recognize it
Instantly and put it to use
Even among the desks
And chairs of the office, should
It come between nine and five.

KABBALAH

Keen As Breath

Black As Law

And Heaven

Moving through darkness, clouds,
And thick darkness.
Returning through darkness, clouds,
And thick darkness.
Some lift up their heels
And some jump.

A MESSAGE FROM RABBI NACHMAN

The extra-human
Swarms with disciples.
Like worms
Tumbling out of the Book of Creation,
The Book of Splendor.
Each with a light
In his head.
But smeared with
The contemplation of ecstasy.

Kabbalah—
A transmission
From mouth to ear.
The words of my friend
Steady my world
Even as I say them.
There are stones—
How else will the house
Be built—
Like souls
That are flung down
In the streets.

LINES FOR ERWIN R. GOODENOUGH
(1893–1996)

"If Aphrodite could take Moses
From the ark in the Nile
In the synagogue at Dura"

Naked as she was
Her breasts blue-pointed

If Aphrodite could move
Among these sheols
Of the dead

If she to ornament the dark
Could bend her body
To the water
Promising life
From the mother

"Come down upon this cup which stands before me,
Fill it with grace and a holy spirit,
So that it becomes for me a new plant within me."

THE KINGDOM

Battering at the door
Of a pretend house
With pretend cries
Of rage and loss
As I sit remembering
Quiet
And dead white.

CROSS COUNTRY

The night's traffic.
I can barely follow the markers,
My eyes stung with seeing.
Snow in the mountains
Is so beautiful.
All through the chemical wastes
Of New Jersey
I follow my guide—
Rare truths in the mountains—
While the kids
Sleep in the back with my wife.
No one to see me
For the dazzling snow.

FIELD MICE

Some wood notes are wild.
Glad to have you in the house,
Piteous small creatures.
Like mad English poets
Of a vanished century,
Something crying to be saved.

HELLO THERE!
for Robert Bly

The poets of the Midwest
Are in their towns,
Looking out across wheat, corn,
Great acres of silos.
Neruda waves to them
From the other side of the field.
They are all so happy
They make images.

DEFINITIONS OF POETRY

1
A practical use
Of mysterious names:
Sun, night, morning, cloud,
Illumination, dreams, love.

2
I want to get out of my skull
For just a little while.
I can't stand the fighting.

3
It's a profitless tit
Said my wife as she put
The baby down.

4
The mist of its own weight.
This striving to wrestle
Myself for a meaning,
Someone must grow tired.

5
I saw myself walking there
Like a bug walking on its shadow
All the way to the dark.

6
The lions are sleeping now
On either side of my forehead,
Keeping the tension in sleep.

ON SOME WORDS OF BEN AZZAI

You will be called by your name.
You will be seated in your place.

You will be given what is yours.
The dream goes something like that
For everyone, I suppose, except
When it's happening and the world
Comes true, the air, the sky.
But all of yesterday and again today
I knew the dream. Age will end it.

SAYINGS OF THE FATHERS

1
Thinking that
In the multiple
Conclusions of a life
There may be
A line truthful
Enough to hand on.

Against the attempt
To create a culture
I place the attempt
To create a life.

This morning
I forgot all about
The continuity
Of American poetry
Engaged on a national mission
Without pay.

2
You think there must be more
To it than this—
A narrow examination
Of a life
A secret poring over books

A listening
For whatever stirs
An intense listening.

3
Peace
Goddess-voice
Keep telling me a story.

A HISTORY

1
You say my thoughts are gestures.
How many times a day
Must I destroy the world?

2
Whatever must rescue me
Will come from outside.
It
Strikes my forehead
Now like the flat
Of a hand.

3
Then it was the time
To take myself seriously again.

To attack the others

To fight for my life.

The stink of non-being
Was on my hands

So I put them to work.

4
Like the fire engine speeding
Out of the firehouse.
The hoarse cry of the last men
As they board her,
As I stare into the wide night,
The nothingness
That gives life.

"THE WAY THINGS ARE"

He is not strong enough
For his experience.
When he cries,
The cat stirs
At the foot of his bed
For a moment.

I tell him
The night's flow—
The traffic and street noises—
Carries sleep.

His dreams
Cannot contain
His experiences.

They go on about him
Like a war
And the poets
Cannot make sense of it.

What is it
That feeds winds and rivers
And the stars?

HOW THE NEWS REACHED ME

My older son was upstairs
Watching a rerun of D Day,
The cannons booming.
I was downstairs
In the dark
Watching the white roses
That had just bloomed—
June 1—against the wall
Of the South Brooklyn
Settlement House.
It was my war
And I sensed it was over.

THANKS AND PRAISE

Because I felt the power
Of what I did not know,
Knew it
As my body tried
Not to know it,
Came that close
To the seizure of stone
And the regression of
Language, saying
The blunt sounds
In my dream
Through iron hinges,
To the level floor
As I cross it,
Thanks and praise.
And want no other thing
Of darkness,
Prince of this world.

TRACTORS

The man was thrown clear
Yet the experts say
To stay in the car is best.
To tap an undercurrent of
Feeling, something I turn away
From, fearful, certain
It will end but not knowing
How it will end.
The dreams have a childish
Beauty.
Fireplaces, planes,
Tractors to clear the roads.

THE ARGUMENT

All right, there are thrones upon thrones.
There is suffering and redemption.
There is exile and return.
But to myself, gripping this pavement?
Thrones upon thrones.
You keep placing them there,
Pyramiding them there
In a golden game.
Art and imagination.
But on this pavement,
In this life, with these eyes?

ALL RIGHT, DOGEN

I let fall
My body and my mind
Into the street,
Watch the world

As pure object
Come back
Like a fist.

IT IS

The smell of enlightenment
Meaning:
I have been there
Before
And brought nothing
Back.

It's a continuity tape
Of the harbor and the bridge
And my life walking past.

In your true and terrible form,
Angel of this world.

FOR DELMORE SCHWARTZ

1
How do they go on living?
How does anyone go on living?
A woman kills her three children
In 1954. In 1966 she kills
Another three. And the husband
Continues to go to work
At the same job. Which
Is to be judged insane?
And we keep walking the same
Roads, past mayhem, slaughter
Of innocents—this morning, the granny
Curled up beside her bottle
Of Petri wine at a side door

Of the Paramount—every day,
Leading sensible lives.
The sirens seem never to stop,
Even in the country, amid
Crickets or ocean sound.
What we all know,
What keeps humming in the back
Of the brain. When the language
Pauses, the killing begins.

2

Your intelligence was so clear
In your first poems, like
Mozart in his music.
Yet it could not help you,
As you said,
When the old arguments,
The din around the family table,
Grew louder all about you—
The arguments we endlessly rehearse
When mind loses its own motion.
Then our jaws lock into the face
We had, on the words we said
Under our breath, to ourselves,
To our underselves, so fiercely deep
They were for years beyond hearing.
And now do all the talking.

3
Disturbed by dreams,
I wake into the chilled morning.
The dreams are rich
With patterns of rejection
(Mother, Wife) suicide and loss.
A victim of such disasters,
When I awake I judge myself
Harshly and long.
Four A.M. on a vacation morning.
The surf takes over in my head, a running
Commentary, a Greek chorus,

Saying something like, nothing but the sea.
In my universe of feeling,
I can hear the sea. These dreams,
Bits of genre, Viennese pastry,
From which I wake, stuffed
With bourgeois living, these dreams
Of the dead fathers I believe in . . .

FROM

Lauds & Nightsounds

1978

THROUGH THE BOROUGHS

I hear the music from the street
Every night. Sequestered at my desk,
My luminous hand finding the dark words.
Hard, very hard. And the music
From car radios is so effortless.
And so I strive to join my music
To that music. So that
The air will carry my voice down
The block, across the bridge,
Through the boroughs where people I love
Can hear my voice, saying to them
Through the music that their lives
Are speaking to them now, as mine to me.

NOTES AT 46

1
What distinguishes our work
Is an American desperation.
Who thought to find this
In the new world?

2
I owe my father a tribute.
On his last day
When the head nurse
Asked what he wanted
He said, I want to
Look into the eyes of a young girl.
The eyes of a young girl.
I want to look into
the eyes of a young girl.

3
It's nothing to me
Who gathers us in.
And it's nothing to me
Who owns us now.
I can think of Venice
Or Jerusalem.
Armand's little goat beard
Quivers in the spring.

4
It suddenly strikes me
That at forty-six
I want to write the lyrics
Of a boy of twenty
So I blow my brains out.

5
Not wanting to invent emotion
I pursued the flat literal,
Saying wife, children, job
Over and over.
When the words took on
Emotion I changed their order.
In this way, I reached daylight
About midnight.

6
"I wish I had never been born!"
He shouts at six.
A pure despair.
At forty-six I cannot say that
With honesty.
Pure passion is beyond me.
Everything is mixed.
Grief allied with joy—
That he is able to say it!

7
In October the house is chill.
Still, the cricket of summer
Sings, reminding us of promises.
As long as the heart listens
It pumps blood.

RIDING WESTWARD

It's holiday night
And crazy Jews are on the road,
Finished with fasting and high on prayer.
On either side of the Long Island Expressway
The lights go spinning
Like the twin ends of my tallis.
I hope I can make it to Utopia Parkway
Where my father lies at the end of his road.
And then home to Brooklyn.
Jews, departure from the law
Is equivalent to death.
Shades, we greet each other.
Darkly, on the Long Island Expressway,
Where I say my own prayers for the dead,
Crowded in Queens, remembered in Queens,
As far away as Brooklyn. Cemeteries
Break against the City like seas,
A white froth of tombstones
Or like schools of herring, still desperate
To escape the angel of death.
Entering the City, you have to say
Memorial prayers as he slides overhead
Looking something like my father approaching
The Ark as the gates close on the Day of Atonement
Here in the car and in Queens and in Brooklyn.

FOR THE YIDDISH SINGERS IN THE LAKEWOOD HOTELS OF MY CHILDHOOD

I don't want to be sheltered here.
I don't want to keep crawling back
To this page, saying to myself,
This is what I have.

I never wanted to make
Sentimental music in the Brill Building.
It's not the voice of Frank Sinatra
I hear.

To be a Jew in Manhattan
Doesn't have to be this.
These lights flung like farfel.
These golden girls.

IN BROOKLYN HARBOR

In Brooklyn harbor
The last light hits the tugs
And Battery shines,
And no one wants to
Make the City any more.

"The Oriental Warrior"
Riding in the bay.

Gulls between the sun
And Governors Island.
Jehovah's Watchtower
With the Squibb tripos
Ever golden. We play
Basketball in the park
Along the harbor. The Bridge
Still stands, getting ancient
With its freight of poetry.

"JESUS, MARY I LOVE YOU SAVE SOULS"

IRT graffiti
For the five o'clock rush hour.
Souls in the car.
Carrying you in my head.
Your head thrown back,
Legs parted. Jesus, Mary
Save souls. I love you.
When we get
To the dark part
Of the ride, under the river,
Keep me in that light,
Subway car light,
Burning forever
With that image
In my brain.

FOR THE SPARROWS ON NEW YEAR'S MORNING

Resolved that I will help feed you in your ivy
And listen for you in the streets
Now that I have heard you, first sound of the year
After the harbor hootings. This morning,
Blurred as the ends of sleep,
You make my resolutions clear, touching on song:
To celebrate without cause whenever
I can put words to sense and music.
And to whoever hears me, let her know
I listen to sparrows.

DISTANCES

She has a kind of grainy beauty
Like one of those square-thumbed,
Slab-footed Greek maidens of
Picasso. So when I see her
I think of sand and sea.

My life on the empty beaches
Just starting to come back.
All the way home we sang
Songs of the '40s and '50s—
"Reeked with class"—
And the kids broke up.
Sometimes they worry
About the desperate way I drive.

There are these distances.

TRUE

It's true I shed tears
In my forties, suddenly,
Explaining who I was
Or where I had been.
Almost like my children,
Who I am quick to comfort.
But I let them
Taste their tears.
The years have taught me.

SAUL'S PROGRESS

1
I told my son:
"Stop trying to screw the monkey's tail
Into his bellybutton.
Originality
Is never its own
Justification.
Some innovations
Get nowhere."

"The Sunday monkeys are my friends,"
He said.
I was on my way down
From the heavenly city
Of the 18th-century philosophers.
He was on his way up.
Almost three.

2
"Moby Dick is smarter than
The other dicks."
A song to make the
Bad guys happy.
You sang it all day Saturday
With snot-filled nose
And clouded eye,
To raise me
To a fury.

3
You sit on the crest of a dune
Facing the sea,
Which is beyond sight.
Your anger at me
Makes you play by yourself,
Tell stories to yourself,
Fling out your hurt
To the wide sky's healing.

A red boat in one hand,
A blue in the other,
You begin singing songs
About the weather.
Cliff swallow, brilliant skimmer.

4
As if he were me, he comes bounding in,
All happiness. I owe him
All happiness. For these years at least.
When he smiles and says, a good time,
I have no notion who else
He has made happy with my happiness.

BRINGING UP KIDS

He goes into paroxysms of grief.
I am baffled by his non-communication,
Knowing perfectly well everything
His rage means to the shaking house.
Disorder at night. It is natural.
He wants to know why it is right.

VETERAN

1
I never thought I'd be a survivor
And base everything on that strategy.
Closing in on fifty, almost un-American,
Out of it, I'm close to myself again
In my fifty-mission photo—
Poised in leather jacket, parachute harness,
By the twin guns of the bomber—
Breathing now,
Twenty, numb, a survivor.

2

To open myself to the wars,
The TV newsreels,
The savage fighting.
To walk with this knowledge,
To see light in this light.
Which was my own youngness.
The shell exploding under the fuselage.
Smoke drifting though the cabin.
Hearing the shell, smelling the smoke.
Knowing it is fire. Making that knowledge
Be with me in the everyday.
Opening my eyes to the sunlight,
Frozen, the condition of my will.
Looking through that to my childhood,
My children.

3

Frozen and baffled,
There is nothing
To be gained
From searching that time.
If one had an answer—
How use it?
Instead, there is the victory
Of being here
With what one has
Like the world itself
That lives
Through time.

EVERY DAY

It's my own dread existence
Stalking me now with a spiritual fury
Like some beast from
Twenty thousand fathoms down
Rammed into the world by events
I seem not to have noticed.

MUSE POEM

While I'm waiting for the words,
Could you just
Lean over me a little,
That way,
With your breasts
Of imagination, incense,
And blue dawns.

It is always the same quiet night.
You in your desperation say,
"What you are writing is poetry.
No one will read it."
You worry about my health
When I find I am not
To be famous. But I am
Already inside you in my thoughts.

IN THE ROOM

Seeing the figure of that man
Caught in a desperate hatred,
I wept for him openly
Before the children,
And I write of him in a low style
But touching on elevated things.

In the room
Nothing has happened
Yet the two of them
Stand apart, watching a ship
Wreck, a wild storm,
Their own blood drumming.

Her hatred of him
Makes her eyes shine,
Brings color to the points
Of her fingers and her hair.

Before we knew about urban poetry
I opened the door and found you
Bathing in the sink, on Stanton Street—
1949—your skin still gleaming.

I can't sleep.
Love has fixed my head.
Now this girl, now that.

Who needs this tumult?
I ask myself,
So proud of the hours
I spend staring.

Muse,
Once you made this chaos shine.

ARRIVING

The way tunnel workers got the bends
In Warner Bros. Movies
I am caught
In the tensions of you.

Describing
Walt Frazier's play
The kid says
So many moves!
And I think of you
In our last season.

Here I am, with
An armful of platitudes
At your door. That
You are never in
Makes my style.

MONTAUK HIGHWAY

Murderous middle age is my engine.

A NOTEBOOK

At the bare edge
The images seem fabulous.

I certainly didn't
Wear myself out
With brilliance.

"It is forbidden to be old" (Nachman)

If you steam blast the bricks
In Brooklyn, they will
Come up as bright as Henry James.

Dead Indians are in the underbrush
Waiting for the word.

I don't like you
And I don't know
Anyone else.

The stars be hid
That led me to this pain.

I stroke my wife's angel hair
Thinking of you.

It is a bowl of blue light.
It will be there all day
Now that I have seen it.

I take out my old anxieties
And they still work.

A notebook of dry cunts.

Why is everything discussed
With that high cackle?
Ladies, I weep for beauty
And you bear it.

I used to visit bombed out towns.
Now I visit bombed out people.
There's a kind of beautiful smell
To both, which I can't
Put out of my mind.

Man, the master of choice.

Words, rushing into judgment.

All right, you mother stickers,
This is a fuck up.

IN OUR DAY

Society
Turning its past
To glorious junk,
Like the artist,
In our day.
Free-floating
Liberation
As a style
In the street.
Everybody
Playing
In the muck
Of the imagination,
Finger-painting
The walls
For psychic health.
The mind's rigor
Become a sunlit field.

HOW DIFFERENCES ARISE

He thinks we live in Rome
Before the coming of Caesar.
He worries about
The health of the Republic.
I know we live in China
Sometime before the coming
Of Confucius.
I find his ideas ridiculous.

JANIS

Seeing you again
I cried for the time
I spent, misspent,
In the rain,
Drinking the booze of confusion.
Ah you, and your ball and chain.
Heels lifted, tugging
At my sentimental heart
Like I was your big daddy
Who wasn't there.
I did drop tears for you,
Coming out of my own generation.
Poster art is what
Hart Crane said we were all about.
American tears for thee.

ADAPTATION OF A FIRST-GRADE COMPOSITION

I suppose I used you
The way an Indian used his buffalo.

I have come in your queenly cunt,
Your tight asshole of an Indian princess.
Buffalo skin for the tepees,

Blankets, pants, and moccasins.
Bones to make tools and drumsticks.
Teeth to make necklaces and anklets.
Skulls to make masks.
And they ate the buffalo meat.

IN FEAR OF FAILURE

1

Facing myself in a long corridor.
A hotel, shoes outside every door.
The light steady, so I can't tell
If it is day or night.
Myself coming toward me,
Murder in the eyes,
The hands trying to form an instrument.
And I sit here before the keys
Remembering when the letters
Were instruments of creation.

2

I see you stand
In the presence of the nouns,
The great shining of the worlds.
You who are as far from me
As thought.

As if a door had been opened
That I could not
Keep open.
Even so
I write the words.

3

Opening the matches
On my desk I read "Your instructor
Is but minutes away."
I sit patiently
Pen in hand
Though it is only
The U.S. Auto Club
Addressing me
And I've been
Driving unsuccessfully
For twenty years.

4
If a world
Still exists
Lights flashing
Like a city
Or a great ship
Going down.

5
I wake from the images.
I have been sleeping with a girl
Half my age. In the light
The engines are moving the day
Into position.

6
Telling the way
One has gone oneself
Or describing a way
Which leads there.

If that will help us.

Complete darkness.

7
The rain for its own sake
So slowly on the roof,
Easing the world,
Even my own anger.
And a solitary bird
Near the house keeps
Telling me what he needs
To tell me: Your drama
Has been played out.

FOR THE YEAR'S END

Staying indoors
At the year's end.
The garden still so green
Against the brick.
The young willow
Set in the cold air
Like an open hand.
Music
Driving me to the year's end
Which I choose,
Turn to now, wanting
To be in
These streets
By the river and the bridge.
I can hardly understand
What holds the music.
A city
Above the water.
Stone holding the music.
Ivy on the wall
In winter.

CITY PORTRAIT

Her husband didn't give her highs,
Just made her lows less low.
Said, with the lips trembling.
Breasts too, I think.
Beautiful woman.
Going to bed with strangers now.
Trying to think it all out.
On the west side of Manhattan,
Twelve floors above the murderous streets.

A GIFT

She made him a gift of her touch,
Softly turning the collar of his jacket down
In the crowded elevator. To say,
See, my spirit still hovers to protect.

That he could prize such useless moments.

Motorbikes break the night's silence.
The President's face on the television screen.
Green on my set. Words muffling perception.
Everything keeps us from the truth, which
Begins to have a religious presence.
Why so many claim it, in the tail of the tiger
Or elsewhere. No matter. When I find it,
Being so rare, it is fiercer than whiskey.
My eyes burn with happiness and I speak
Collected into myself.

LIKE A BEACH

Even the unlived life within us
Is worth examining.
Maybe it is all we have.
The rest is burned up
Like fuel in the furnace.
But the unlived life
Stretches within us like a beach.
There is a gull's shadow on it.
Or it is at night and the moon
Crusts the sand.
Or it is a house at night
With people talking in the next room
Over cards. You believe
In these observations?
Doesn't the sea sweep in,
The action begin in the house

At night, the voices of the players
Loud in argument,
Their motives, their needs,
Turbulent as the sea?
Whose happiness
Even here
Is being sacrificed?

AUGUST

1
Ancient mariner, your gray beard
Dries in the sun, salt sparkling
The wires. Beached on this vacation coast,
You have forgotten your story.
It's drifted away among children,
Scrub pine, the chattering sea.
And there is no one to hold
By the eye or sweet tit anyway.
Better to whistle with the birds,
And pick berries in the sun.

2
I can begin to taste my life,
The wine's sweet influence.
Surf or traffic, I can't tell.
When you begin, stars cluster on the vine.
You walk through a meadow.
You stand casting from an open boat
Into Scorpio. Soft chalk
In the sky because it is mid-August
And the time of Perseids.
Now am I home in Helicon,
The real estate I was meant to keep.

MUSICAL SHUTTLE

Night, expositor of love.
Seeing the sky for the first time
That year, I watched the summer constellations
Hang in air: Scorpio with
Half of heaven in his tail.
Breath, tissue of air, cat's cradle.
I walked the shore
Where cold rocks mourned in water
Like the planets lost in air.
Ocean was a low sound.
The gatekeeper suddenly gone,
Whatever the heart cried
Voice tied to dark sound.
The shuttle went way back then,
Hooking me up to the first song
That ever chimed in my head.
Under a sky gone slick with stars,
The aria tumbling forth:
Bird and star.
However those cadences
Rocked me in the learning years,
However that soft death sang—
Of star become a bird's pulse,
Of the spanned distances
Where the bird's breath eddied forth—
I recovered the lost ground.
The bird's throat
Bare as the sand on which I walked.
Love in his season
Had moved me with that song.

TIGHT LIKE THAT

Who can refuse to live his own life?
A spray of leaves in the lamplight.
A saxophone on the dark street.

Like the forties. In those days
For the price of a pitcher of beer
You could spend Saturday afternoon
Listening to the exchanges,
The deep guttural stirrings
Of so much light and dark.
At the corner of fifty-second
At the break at the Downbeat
We saw Billie draped in fur,
Gardenia in her hair.
Bless you, children, she said.
Whatever became of the music
I drank to at Nick's bar,
Pee Wee Russell's clarinet
Jammed into Brunes's belly,
Shaking like his sister Kate.
Hunkering down into my own story,
I begin to see it all close up.

THE BRIDGE

for John Wissemann

John, the old bunker fleet at Greenport
Is a ghost. Many beautiful things are gone.
The masts, the dockside buildings
Float in your blue water colors,
Blue and black, in Brooklyn,
Where I seem to be giving up the ghost.
Artists of the region. All one island.
Whitman's funny fish-shaped island.

Like you I do the indigenous stuff—
Crabs from the creek, blues from the September sea,
Poems from the tar roofs and the red brick library
Where they house the prints—opening the Bridge!
Fireworks and exultation! Crowds moving

In a mighty congress back and forth.
While we, unmoving on the starry grid of America,
Stare failure in the face, our blazing star.

It was a dream of summer. From the cliffs above
The Sound—humming birds hovering, red foxes
At the door—at evening I could see the schools
Of blues come in, savaging the waters and the bait.
Everything I wrote was magic to me. Ancient days.
Believe me, John, they wear us down with shit and work.
But one pure line—still mine or yours
For the grasping—can take us to that farther shore.

INCIDENT

1
Tremendous pleasure lurking in my skin.
You stretch, your small breasts announcing,
This is the beginning. If we were to lie together,
I would have to tell you my long story.
Slowly I begin to rehearse it.

2
As a flame is joined to a coal,
That cleaving to the source.
I don't hear from you for ten days.
Still, everyone says I look good.

3
I passed you
Standing at the rail
In the Indianapolis
Speedway of my bankrupt emotions,
Going into the last turn
Before the blossoming fire.
That's me, waving thanks to you,
From under the car.

47TH STREET

In the delicatessen
The countermen
Were bantering about the messiah,
Lifting the mounds of corned beef
And tongue. He wouldn't come,
They said, you couldn't
Count on it. Meaning:
They would die in harness.

IN THE SYNAGOGUE

The new year. Five thousand what?
God's deliberate flatness
In his scrolls, with touches of
Megalomania and song.

BROOKLYN GARDENS

Forsythia, scraggly in the backyard.
Crocuses, stabs of blue in the shadow.
Sentiment, blundering now like the trucks.
Even in myself I see mysterious purposes.

NIGHTSOUNDS

I
My fingers bear the marks
Of fish hooks, puppy bites,
All the sweet bites of the actual.
You, goddess, who grab me

Between the second drink and the third,
I now see like me
For the marks I carry on me.

2
As if the night were a problem
I had to crack
To let the dawn through.

3
It is near bedtime
And suddenly I am stunned
By the gold of the whiskey in my glass.
I cannot understand
Why so much has been given.

4
He was looking for a
Universal message like,
Hemorrhoid sufferers
You are not alone.

5
You throw one leg
Over the covers.
A gleam of snatch
In the half light.

6
I have long been a man
Of filthy habits.
And now in middle age
They give me pleasure.

7
I am watching another
Man's defeat.
It seems

He cannot bring himself
To it
While I watch.

8
Where you stand
There stand all the worlds.

9
What is this sweetness
I am overcome by
As if I had earned
My rest.

DOMESTIC MATTERS

It wasn't what I had thought—
Children taking up
Most of the house, leaving
Me (or so it often seems)
Only room enough
For the bed. Which itself
Is a kind of relic, as if
From an earlier
Marriage. And so you turn
In the bedroom door,
White, and so small,
To say goodnight.
To say there are
Two of us.

I am crying over this body of yours
Which is to wither in the dust.
Already your belly's thrust outpoints
Your breasts. The hair of your head
Grows thin. A skeleton
Smiles to me with your gums.

We are almost
Out of earshot
Of one another
Yet our answers
Seem to find
Connected questions
Of an urgency
So deep, they might
Be coming
From the center
Of a life.

We were comrades
In a disastrous war.
We have created a history
That will be sung
In the psyche of others.
Troy's burning
And the flames may light us
All the way to death.

CRY OF THE SMALL RABBITS

The cry of the small rabbits facing death.
Nobody would want to sing like that.
A short, high wailing. So what
If death gave them voice to sing?
I face my own rage and fear, tearing for words
That I can say calmly in sentences
That will not stop. I want to see
The next line glitter, and the last
Come crashing like surf.

FOR THE ZEN MASTER SKATEBOARDING DOWN INDEPENDENCE PASS

The upturned soles of Buddha's feet.
He was not himself anymore.
That happiness.

Mind-racing
The green hills, blue
Mountain daisies.

Freedom of the downward glide,
Swallows' wings, overdrive.
Knees bent for the turn
As the mountain turns.

MUFFDIVING ON THE UPPER WEST SIDE

Not only was I there, in the rooms,
But when night cradled those bodegas
I saw the music ripple like stars.

O SEASONS

1
It seemed reasonable to expect an answer.
That was an early feeling, like owning something.
Urban dawn, and yet to hear the birds.
I must have that happiness.

2
Speculations about man's soul:
A face within a face,
The transformer, the perfecting agent
In the disassembled gear I carry
With me into day. Crossing the street

Steam flurries from the underground.
My life as hidden as the godhead
On 43rd and Broadway where garments
Of light wrap the tall buildings
And I step forth, fierce to know.

3

Excuse this boy from life
I wanted my mother to write
As I went off to school.
It would take a cosmic jubilee
To make my soul ascend
From this despair. If I could say
My native home, and turn
In that direction, glass in hand,
Crossing the crowded room
As once I came to you.
These misinformed meditations
Hurrying the world's
Return to waste and void.

4

So I come home
And the gay guy next door
Is singing Hawaiian songs
In a contralto. His job
Must be as tough as mine.

5

It's true I was timid
On my way to Esau in the Sixties.
Someone said, "The place to which we are going
Is not subject to any law,
Because all that is on the side of death;
But we are going to life." It was
Her heart-shaped ass made me do it.
Descriptions of wreckage. The blown windows
Of a town house in Manhattan.
Fucking in the desert.

6

Wind in the leaves along the street.
Another year is hurried to its close.
Today I passed a man struck down
On 33rd street. Yesterday,
On the steps of the Borough Hall station
I saw another gone, eyes open
To the sifting, grayish light.

7

Bordering on vacancy at the year's end.
The whole continent unpeopled.
The created uncreate. The monuments
Crawled back into cold stone. The thick husks.
One thousand nine hundred and seventy-seven
Years of Christendom, dumb in this believer,
Cherishing the light to come on the bleak
Cityscape—vacant lot on the street
To Jehovah's Kingdom, by the peerless bridge.

ANCIENT DAYS

Great things had happened.
They felt called upon
To bear witness.
The words, in themselves,
Became events.

1976

Vision floats
Over the death camps.
That stink. Till the end
Of history. Not soteriology
Or the American sublime
Can raise man up.

Magnified and sanctified.
The fallen sparks,
Husks, on the street corners,
In the streets.

PORTRAIT

At forty-six,
His wife committed again,
His two children
Only babes, he couldn't
Even contemplate divorce.
Yet the women were there—
Young women, the wealth
Of the city. He worked
At his job, still dreaming
Of the novel. Saloon dreams,
He said, Irish, you can't
Live without them.

POETS & COMICS

To make a little noise before death.

THE REALIZATION

If one could follow a man
Through the places of his exile,
Asking him at each point
Why he had strayed from his life
Or been turned from it,

In time the dialogue
Would be meaningless
For the exile would be the life.
So we live.

THE OLD WIFE SPEAKS

What he needs
Are six call girls,
Each with her own
Cocksucking techniques.
Meanwhile, he brings me
His laundry.

VACATION POETRY

1
An inexhaustible day but in the end
There were no prizes. I sharpened
Into seeing a few times, before
And after whiskey. The beach was
One great sunlit navel.
The sea, like a medieval gloss, moved
On four levels. I walked east along
The tide mark, the spent text.

2
This air is made of bird calls,
Telephone wires, blue sky and clouds.
It has a disarming honesty. Peanut butter
Would not spread as evenly.
I have come to think of my daydreams of you,
Seventeen porno movies with one plot,
As a waste of time. The longitudes
Of my indifference begin to envelope space.

3

How difficult it is to acknowledge
This is what I'm here for. A furniture
Mover might have a stronger sense of mission.
In combat I understood the value of survival
And the necessity for strict attention.
In life's miasma, I drift apart.
Even when she looks toward me
My moves tend to be comical.

4

"The great elementary principle of pleasure"
By which man "knows and feels, and lives, and moves."
I'll drink to that, said Brustein,
Smacking his lips. For the fourth time today
I swim in the sea. Butterflies pass me
On my bike, as do bikinied women,
Strutting in their cream and brown. Voluptuous
Pages from Keats and Baudelaire.

AFTER DARK

Day's end. The promise of day ended.
A rehearsal to say goodnight.
But peaceably so, after whiskey or love.
Not after pain, not often after pain.

LINES

Blue darkening. A bar of it.
Dan calls to say he'll be home by ten;
Do I mind if he's out that late.
I smoke a cigar, study the page,
Cherish the silence. My paint-
Smeared pants pronounce me
The captain of good works.

Happy homesteader, husband.
So I never trafficked in guns
In Africa. And I became myself
And not another. My own vacillations
Rampant in my lines.
Responsibility on my abraded shoulders.
Singer of neurasthenia, or something like it,
Was my aim. What wings touch
Me now out of the darkening blue?

THE INTENSITY

When you think over what she said and what you said
The spaces begin to get larger until they modulate
Into silence. You stand there staring at each other
With no balloons floating the words, no
Captions, only the intensity of sight making
A language to scare anyone interested in communication
Or believing that two human beings can connect.
Which is why my happiness on the subway brings me back
To myself after last night's trouble. The body warmth,
The distended-with-sleep faces, the memories
Of Hart Crane riding this line, tunneling this way
Under the river that is east. Next time
When I beg for something, will you recognize
Need, stop talking, stop closing the door.

HAPPINESS IN DOWNTOWN BROOKLYN

This morning
Twenty gospel singers
Roared inside my head.

Happiness
In downtown Brooklyn.

All the solid buildings
Were as bright as clouds.

FROM A CHINESE MASTER

1
If you want to enter the room
You have to say something. You cannot
Take it for granted that you have already
Entered the room. This I want
To point out to you with a smile.

2
Early Sunday. Under the phosphor glare
Birds sing merrily, twigs bud.
A dream pushed me from my bed
Breathing of promise like this April.
Believe me, said the teacher in my dream,
A single true gesture, if it be
Only that of the big toe, is enough.

3
The glamour of death is on their heads.
Wanderers in the anthologies.
After the job I sit with beer and bourbon.
In what cold light shall we be one?

4
At the start and at the finish
What we want
Is to be close to the living,
Our heads against the skin of the song.

DITCH PLAIN POEM

To be there when day breaks on the sea's reaches.
The full moon still hung there. At Ditch Plain,
For example, before the surfers appear.
Water over rock and gravel. Shingle sound.
Beautiful enough in this end of July
Drought of fish to make me stand there,
Hungry for a text—in the water, on the sand.
Something to bring back to my desk like
Beach glass or polished stone. I want
My happiness to be visible.
I want to bless this day with meaning.
Let the rest of my life take care of itself
So long as it can hover there.

The Light Holds

1984

THINGS SEEN

There is no natural scenery like this:
when her loose gown from her shoulders
falls, the light hardens, shadows
move slowly, my breath catches.

The flame of the blue cornflower,
a half inch above the flower,
fanned by wind.

FROM THE GREEK ANTHOLOGY

Darling, start at any point you wish.
How kind I was to myself in those days,
and so happy cataloguing ships.
Your lovely way of walking and the radiance of your face.
The Cyprian goddess set these before me.
The rest I accomplished on my own.

THE TWIG

from the Yiddish of Joseph Rolnick

A man plants a stick,
pats the dirt
and says, Mine.
Now he is committed,
let him pray for sun and rain.
Each night he covers miles
for the sake of that naked twig,
and in the morning
runs to it as fast.
He is worn out with worry
and waits for his last days.
But how that stick
branches in his mind—

a mighty tree,
full of shade,
where years later he can sit
in the middle of the day
as the sun grows warm.

JULY

You poets of the Late T'ang send me messages this morning.
The eastern sky is streaked with red.
Linkages of bird song make a floating chain.
In a corner of the world, walled in by ocean and sky,
I can look back on so many destructive days and nights,
and forward too, ego demons as far as mind reaches.
Here, for a moment, the light holds.

MAY 14, 1978

The poet Miyazawa Kenji asks me,
What world is it you want to enter?
Percussive rain on the early morning window.
The house, the steady breathing, focused now
on the lighted surface of my desk.
I cannot answer him for joy and dread.

CITY

Silver dawn over Madison Avenue.
The refrigerator shuts softly, like a kiss.

He is dying of the terminal cutsies
she says of the cultural journalist,
the newspaper spread before her on the table.
Thousands fail in her sight daily.

The word "happiness"
like the sun in late March
is a light I can see
but not feel. There it is
on the back of my hand
as real as my hand
clenched now
against the wind on 48th Street.

In Great Neck, at 4:30 in the morning,
Ring Lardner and Scott Fitzgerald
walk the streets. American success
is their theme. The sleepers drink it in
across the lawns.

In the lamp's circle,
warmed by bourbon,
I play the role out. It is
not to tell the world
anything. What is it
the world would want to know?

Her furious body, plunged into sleep.
On the pillow, her live hair,
helmet and cloak. What I say in the room
is for me and the walls. We are doing darkness,
each in his own way.

THE CARD

Closed in by the rain, the February chill,
he looks at her card sent from an island
in the sun. She writes, "The vasts and deeps
of the mistakenness of this undertaking
remain to be measured." What he drinks
can't begin to fill his emptiness
or banish the chill. Only the pen seems warm.
Is she warning him of her vision of their

condition? Possibly. She writes,
"I'm having funny dreams, you and I
in Paris. Also you and my mother
married. And others." When she comes back
he will begin to batter at her indifference
again. She does not sign love, just
"Pray for me" and the initials of her name.

THE WISH

This night in Brooklyn is as ancient
as nights get, though the moon
hangs like a lamp, and the traffic
slurs in my room.
My desire is as sharp as whiskey
or a hurt nerve, from my head
to my hand: to populate
the void, to turn this blankness
into a field of stars, where I can sleep
forever in my earned sleep,
comforted by the wind off Atlantic
Avenue, and the waters at its end.
Lights rise from the water, a City
across the way, that I raise
in my empty room to starlight.

MIDDLE CLASS

Whatever happened to the screaming-meemies?
I see my life has surfaced once again.
She explained to me on the phone
all the things I had to live for.
It came to three items. Not enough.
I spent one hour with one son at his shrink
discussing (my choice) why he seemed to hate me.
Because I'm insensitive and unfeeling, he said.

The shrink said it wasn't hate but anger.
We all agreed to discuss it again.
If I get up when the alarm rings tomorrow,
I can pay for the hour and all the hours.
On the subway I see nobody finds it easy.
As beautiful as you are, you're not enough.

LEARNING

1
He is back in a student's room
having learned nothing
in 35 years, except
despair and happiness are sweeter
to him now, they are purer
to his taste, as if he had
learned to discriminate among
his emotions, to say this is
despair and this is happiness:

2
Paying dues—
you imagine this is
a creative loneliness.
You are aware of wind
or traffic rushing in
the street. You think
God is as lost as you:
the fixed points vanished,
the beginning and the end
both forgotten. Day
after day the light
is its own explanation.

3
In my room a bug climbs the white wall
or rather seems to be thinking of climbing it.
I too would like to get to the top of something.

From *The Light Holds,* 1984   ❖   139

4
Rabbi Nachman's final message:
Gevalt! Do not despair!
There is no such thing as despair at all!
Shouted from the very depths of the heart.

SAN FRANCISCO

In this western city, under cloud cover,
the lives are ranged about me on the hills,
no more obscure to me than in Manhattan.
Downtown, a writer gets up from his desk
to check the Bay Bridge and the white sails
against blue water. What is always there,
out the window, is the failure I feel
before America, my inability to make it rhyme
with my interior weather, except
under the stress of strong emotion —
love or loss—when I know
my father is stumbling home,
tired after work, carrying his family
in his heart to whom he promises
happiness and all bright things,
and he stops in a store
to bring me, sick in bed, a giant
locomotive to take me there.

SUMMER AND BACK

1
Pearl-gray dawn over the sea's margin.
A few terns against the lit sky to the east.

2
Bird clickings in the sheltered grove.
On the wires, bird identification

like aircraft identification.
My life depends on it.

How the reaching back, over 30 years,
takes place effortlessly. Grace of memory,
though the affect is dolorous,
knits up the mind.

3
Closing your door
I feel some great erotic mystery
slipping away—
Phil Spitalny's All-Girl Orchestra,
the show over, descending
into the pit.

4
Recognizing the real, as in the undersong
I heard when the blonde, with open throttle,
ran over "The Man I Love" and the backup pianist
with that genuine pallor of a man
who has never been outside by day
riffed through the pauses and the bourbon
tasted like it did 20 years ago.
As if the sentimental were not real. Starlight
after the neon of the roadhouse, a windshield
full of stars.

5
Absolute blue bearing down on me
makes me swerve into thoughts of you.
That earth softness, wetness, foliage
thick enough to hide me in a room
like any other in the city.

6
I come to you
as a poor man
comes to the table of the rich,

ill at ease
and determined
to enjoy it.

7
In my fifties
I discovered fish too fierce
for my equipment. They took
all my bait. A bare hook
became my emblem.

ON A SUNDAY

When you write something
you want it to live—
you have that obligation, to give it
a start in life.
Virginia Woolf, pockets full of stones,
sinks into the sad river
that surrounds us daily. Everything
about London amazed her, the shapes
and sights, the conversations on a bus.
At the end of her life, she said,
London is my patriotism.
I feel that about New York.
Would Frank O'Hara say, Virginia Woolf,
get up? No, but images from her novels
stay in my head—the old poet,
Swinburne, I suppose, sits on the lawn
of the country house, mumbling
into the sun. Pleased with the images,
I won't let the chaos of my life
overwhelm me. There is the City,
and the sun blazes on Central Park
in September. These people, on a Sunday,
are beautiful, various. And the poor
among them make me think

the experience I knew will be relived again,
so that my sentences will keep hold
of reality, for a while at least.

DISCOVERY

When I wake
in the early hours
I think there must be
something I have learned
from these violent dreams
and then I know
how it will be
in my last hours.

CUMMINGS

On May nights, in Patchin Place,
Greenwich Village of my memory,
girls from Smith and Vassar
vagabonding for the weekend,
lovely in the alley light,
would chant up to the shy poet's
window: How do you like your blue-
eyed boy, Mr. Death. And indeed
Buffalo Bill's defunct—pencil-thin
by the alley gate, sketchbook in hand,
open collar of the artist, across
from the Women's House of Detention
in the waning light of afternoons.

From *The Light Holds,* 1984   ❦   143

SONS

They have what they want.
You're going down
but ready to help.

They touch you sometimes.

What to give them?
Vanish.
Leave a trace.

AUTOBIOGRAPHY

To read by daylight.
To look up and see
on my wall
the print of the plans
for the Brooklyn Bridge,
the pleasure of its being there
with the current of the East River
surging underneath. Stasis
and flow. Of course. The tension
of the New Critics still feeding
my fifties life.

YEARS AGO

The sky was bright
blue—
the color of birds'
eggs in storybooks.
The print was so large
when my young sons talked.

MOVIE

At the space movie
the galaxies seemed so fine
viewed from aboard
the rocket ship. I didn't want
the trip to end. Out there,
I thought, we could move forever,
without consequence or pain,
just the sensation of flight
and precise tasks to be done.
Everyone on board
knew the story line meant nothing,
the dialogue just air,
pious remnants of an earthly life.

AROUND TOWN

And this is just your everyday pathos.
The handsome young woman
in the white turtleneck
leaves the guy at the table,
enters the phone booth
to cry, silently,
for maybe three minutes,
then dabs twice and returns.

Or the little black girl on the subway
to Brooklyn, clutching
a miniature white doll
in a matchbox cradle—
blond hair, blue eyes—
one hand around the box,
the thumb caressing.

BROOKLYN HEIGHTS

I

I'm on Water Street in Brooklyn,
between the Brooklyn Bridge
and the Manhattan Bridge,
the high charge of their traffic
filling the empty street.
Abandoned warehouses
on either side.
In the shadowed doorways, shades
of Melville and Murder Incorporated.
Five o'clock October light.
Jets and gulls in the fleecy sky.
Climbing the hill to Columbia Heights,
I turn to see the cordage
of the Brooklyn Bridge, and behind it
the battle-gray Manhattan.

2

This room shelved high with books
echoes with my midnights. Pages
of useless lines swim in it. Only
now and then a voice cuts through
saying something right: No sound
is dissonant which tells of life.
The gaudy ensigns of this life
flash in the streets; a December light,
whipped by wind, is at the windows.
Even now the English poets are in the street:
Keats and Coleridge on Hicks Street
heading for the Bridge. Swayed aloft there,
the lower bay before them, they can
bring me back my City line by line.

WINTER SUN

Shakespeare in Central Park in winter,
bare ruined choirs behind him,
a green figure, in green livery,
clutching a book. Afternoon sun
no higher than the Gulf and Western
building. Rags of the departing year
in my head, the lived with
but not understood events that I
have worn thin through worry.
If only the imagination rayed from the bard's
head, from behind his sunken eyes—
if those eyes were zap guns of the imagination
transforming the unusable past into energy,
bunched light waves stronger than
this winter sun that shows me who I am
against bare trees and a sullen sky.

BAD NEWS

1
There is a bag lady who has her station
on 43rd Street near Sixth Avenue,
in the middle of the sidewalk. She was there
when I went to work, and there on my return.
The New York Times and *The New Yorker*
are on that street. So is the Century Club.
It's a hard street to impress, I want
to tell her, even with bags of different colors
and scarves to examine slowly in the sun.

2
Death won't claim you. Nothing
as dramatic as that.
You'll just go off the edge, roll
off it, like falling out of bed.
They can tell from the sound.

3
She opens for the telephone
more than for me.
The laughs keep getting
deeper, keep coming
and the breath . . .

4
What can these clouds tell me—
I am so hooked on the day to day—
when they sail over
like lofty propositions.

5
Subway cars roll in
each like a Gauguin jungle
with messages for the city
from the city: "This is
energy from my soul"
and "United Artists."

6
The local prophet,
bearded, wearing skins in summer,
dropped a potted plant in the middle
of 79th Street and Madison Avenue
and walked on. Tires crunched
on the shards, and flowers
bloomed in the headlights.

7
There are other realities
I keep telling the world.
Why do I rage when I say it?
Because there is the one reality
that I cannot bring myself to say.

8
These stars have no significance.
As it turned out
I didn't know enough
to find my way home.

A MEMORIAL

My mother and father on the town,
in the photograph. American jazz
in the swing of her handbag
banging from her wrist.
Spats, and the woman
with a rose in her hair.
Hey, this was
a big romance. He was making money,
going to make more money. Everything
was looking up.
I love them in this photograph.

BLUE EYES

Young women with the baby fat
still on them, smelling of milk.
Against that, her bravery—
striding out of bed in the morning,
her years, her children underfoot,
her blue eyes flashing warning.

"I could make some of these guys very happy,"
she said, looking up from the personals
in the *New York Review of Books*.

You read to her of war,
devastation, gut-chilling
insecurity, and her blue eyes
waver, and she sleeps
like an American child.

"Is this a peak experience?"
she said, sliding down beside him,
her blue eyes laughing at his desperate age.

Sound of surf through dense fog.
Moisture streaming from the screened windows.
"Where are the beautiful love poems?"
she keeps asking him.

She became the line
he had in his head
just before sleep, that
he thought he would retain
and now it's gone.

INTERLUDE

He had his own prescription for entering
the life of his times.
This was what everything drifted to
inexorably: His hand
on the small of her back.

She spoke about the special
loneliness of the city.

She said, lay down your arms, nothing
will come of this but more tears, more
unhappiness, on which you fatten and grown dull.
Enjoy the streets. The rain is
your proper element. Stop trying to light fires
where damp ashes are what is meant.

Goddess, destroyer, flaming-haired,
whiskey-throated,
the small birds keep their distance
when you walk across to me.

AT THE SHORE

1
The bugs batting against the lamp, the midges,
in an old house, in summer,
the peacefulness after voices are stilled
is like the still small voice we were
told to tune into as children.

2
If you could figure it out,
the domestic arrangements you fall into,
like beds or a summer at the shore.
You wake up facing a meadow,
beyond that water, beyond that an island.
On the other side of the island
you begin another life.

3
The big dipper is outside my door,
so I can find my way north,
if that is the way I need to go.
For the moment I am content
to drink and smoke and stroke
the inside of your thighs
that have taken on the smoothness
of beach glass, glazed by the sea,
a remembrance.

4
The man who has no talent for relationships
listens to the wind. It comes sweeping off
the harbor and the bay into the blue room.

He thinks he can recognize
every tune it plays. What
he wants is merciless music, the sound
at the very bottom of the harbor.

5
The chink of the moth
on my glass, the dog's
heavy breathing as if
some race were being run again,
and my own solitary presence
at my desk are all emblems
for me of the night world.
In the next room
you sprawl in sleep
so that my day can begin again.

6
Night after night
the wind is from the south,
off Shelter Island, wisps
of lightning play about the sky.
Orienting myself by that speaking wind,
I rise, troubled in lamplight,
to say once again that my
dreams are pernicious
and blur the clarity of what I see—
mute swans, cormorants, the rushes.
This self, this consciousness, this pressure cooker
for rhetoric and bad vibes
that I lug to the country.
It is my usual hour—3 A.M.
When I was younger and had the gift of sight
I did not understand that all that is asked
is that we not mar the work of creation,
doing injury to others and ourselves.

HOW IT IS WITH ME

In my luxuriant cool,
after a bit of weed and
a little coffee, I go out
among the moving slim waists
of the Upper East Side.

GETTING THROUGH THE DAY

The old woman
humming, coming
up the subway steps,
one hum
for each step.

BATTLEMENTS

for H. R. Hays

These dark colors I place against
the blue heron at Louse Point. Summer
eternal, though after we go,
it may all be paved over.

Into the calm morning
steps the blue heron. The shore
oscillates like a nest to his leaving.

The old poet is brought down to look at the bay.
He thinks he has never done justice to anything in his poems.
Gulls crack shells on the macadam road.
Returning, held by others, he urinates by the car.

When you die, who will come out
to meet you if not the blue heron.

FOR WILLIAM DUNBAR AND HIS LAMENT

Sir, the words have prevailed, though readers are few.
In the early morning I lament with you, and take comfort
    from you
that some have found the way to fix their name.
In your trim stanzas, noble in their naming of others,
you hold fast to light, and are access to light for others,
for me, in this darkness I cannot strike or leave.

MEMENTO MORI

Suppose you lived across from a funeral home—
say the Frank E. Campbell funeral home
where the stacked dead wait to be delivered
like fresh loaves of bread—would you, each night,
when you rise to the muted windows
look on that day as the last day
but know it is not for you to make
the judgment, it is enough to believe
the judgment is done, sleep peacefully
on that, rise tomorrow as the sun
touches with light the streets and avenues
where you go in search of your life.

CONSIDERING

Like the man who walked
his three-legged dog
in Central Park—
pride and pathos
struggling in his face—
I consider my life
and my art.

CITYSCAPE

The self hurt, humiliated,
has no recourse but to the world.
Dawn's light
on the streets, though
the buildings are still dark.

Sparrows nesting in the hollow crossbar
of the traffic light. A beak
and head emerge, and then the line
of flight, as if city air
could sustain flight.

June and the hum of air conditioners
fills the side streets.
A poster in a Madison Avenue boutique
says Poverty Sucks. The crowd
coming out of the Whitney opening
believes it, so well kept
they shine along the pavement.

Gulls as far inland
as Fifth Avenue.

After the garbage truck
has stopped grinding the world,
the rhetoric inside my head
catches and begins to work.

My eye on the cityscape,
nervous, alert,
as I move through
the day. No part
of the surface
is neutral ground.

THE END

Imagine your own death.
I'm wearing my father's
gray tweed overcoat.
I've just had a corned-beef
sandwich on 47th Street

(I asked for lean
and it came fat,
I should have sent it
back) when it hits me
in the chest.

EXPERIENCES

"I've been there before!"
shouted like the prophet
when he was lifted up
to behold the burning city
but I was going down
into the subway for my
first vision of the day.

In the hospital I heard a voice say,
"The chart has to accompany the patient,"
which used to be true in our universe
when Kafka wrote and Jews prayed.

When I was mugged
and kicked in the head
by three stalwart blacks
I felt like a gazelle
cut out from the herd
on the deserted subway platform.

In summer I place my one plant
outside. That makes the apartment
seem so bare. But the plant gets spiky,
luminous, and cheers me when
I see it from my bedroom window.
We are beginning to help
each other understand what it is to be
solitary but alive.

Seeing old friends, or even people we've known
a long time who are not friends, simply
people who share a part of our past,
is healing, heals the discontinuities,
permits us to believe that our lives
have grown organically, from there to here,
and that we have not existed in isolated
moments, as different people, caught
in different stories, moving at different speeds,
which is the way we know it to be.

In my apartment everything
suggests the emptiness of Grant's tomb
figuring Grant got out
and nobody got in.

I don't panic anymore
when I wake in the small hours.
I know this time is as real
as any other.

Wanting to make barge music by the Brooklyn Bridge
the way other men want to make love, or be happy,
or take something home to the wife and kids.

Not having known any other life,
this is what one summons.
There is sympathetic understanding,
but the mind is locked in place
by its experience.

He keeps saying "these streets"
and doesn't know
what he means.

The literature of our time, like papers
pushed into the cracks of the wall in Jerusalem,
to be read by an unknown god, when he
returns to consciousness and summons us.

The light streaming from the closed door
of the one letter of the alphabet
I am supposed to say.

A JERUSALEM NOTEBOOK

I
A city of ascensions,
nowhere to go but up.
Forcing the spirit in New York
is the commonplace, we live
there as if we were in Jerusalem,
Jesus and Mohammed touching down
and going up, just another
launching pad, as I get off
the bus and head home.

2. *Postcard*
It is not far from here
that the parents stood
and the child, placed into the priest's machine,
heard the wail
of Moloch. And the bronze god,
arms outstretched, smiled at the smoke.
Two of the kings of Judah
burned their sons here—
Hell, Gehenna, Gai Hinnom,

the pleasant valley of Hinnom,
pink, scarred and silent
in the fading light.

3
If you begin housekeeping
at the edge of Gehenna
you have to expect a little trouble.
She said to me: I like
this place because there are no birds.
No. She said to me: *Actually,*
I like this place because there
are no birds. The white lizard
on the white wall seemed transfixed
by the thought of hell. Looking east
and south I see the Judean hills,
a desert like a sea.
Or dunes dropping off into a sea.
Morning vapors rising off the land.
Give me this place for my own,
I cried, and I will live here forever.
The prospect is as sweet
as a Sabbath morning. Across
the valley of Gehenna cypresses line
the sloping hill. I can walk
there any time I like, now
I am old enough, and look back
on this life I have begun.

4. *Tourists*
She is crying over three olives
that I threw out. Three olives
but my food, she cries. She is
not a child but a woman.
Outside Zion Gate, Jaffa Gate,
Dung Gate, she rubs my arm slowly.
Gates excite her. Where I come in
at night, the city is so beautiful.

5
It is the temple mount.
It is a little like the temple mount,
though I myself constitute
the sightseers, worshippers,
and sometimes the visiting god.

6
Whatever brought me here, to a new moon
over Zion's hill, dark moon
with the thin cusp silvered,
help me believe in my happiness, for
it was guilt that woke me. A voice
on the telephone crying breakdown.
Illusions of my own ego causing destruction
while outside the marvelous
machinery of day has opened, light
traffic on the road to the citadel.
And as I look again, it is all
swept clean, except for
a faint pink in the sky and on the old
stones of the city, and language in my head
that I brought with me, that I carry,
that I use to mark my way.

7
My way of being in the world:
not perfect freedom or the pitch
of madness, but that the particulars
of my life become manifest
to me walking these dark streets.

8. *For C.R.*
When I dropped permanence from my back
and saw what I had taken for
solid buildings and good roads
was desert all about me and within me,
how bright became the sunlight,
how sweet the evening air.

9. *The Old Jewish Poet Floats in* The Dead Sea
It is the lowest place on earth
but he has been lower.
For example, he has been on the heights
of Massada, watching the Roman soldiers
jack off in the baths below.
He knows his turn will be next.
Beneath him floats a crow.
Beneath the crow floats the crow's shadow.
Beneath the crow's shadow is another Jew.
These Judean junk hills
fill his head with sulphur.
Every hill is a hill of skulls.

10

I understand we are like smoke.
It streams from my cigar into the morning air,
silken, prism like in sunlight.
Nothing I do with my life
could be as beautiful.

11

Lizard lines in his skin.
Striving to become one with the stones
like the lizard, even as the pen
darts into the shadow of the page.

12

I have dreams coming out of my ears,
she said. Why not? This city has seen
so many mad dreamers, their stale dreams
even now looking for new homes.
The stones dream in the sun,
the lizards. In the golden mosque,
riots of line and color, shapes dream
in the marble columns, pulsing in
and out of sleep. When the city wakes
the action is brief and bloody.
Let it sleep. Let the garbardined Jews

dream of the Messiah. He approaches
the blocked-off gate of the walled city.
Taste the dream of the Jews.

13
Why did I want to sit out all the time,
was the air so special? Yes,
soft and today dust-blue. But the smell
of corpses had been everywhere, and more to come.
Red buses and blue buses raced the roads
to the small towns, carrying infant Jesuses,
dynamite. Blondes from Scandinavia,
silver-toed, tried on Arab dresses
while the man in the stall scratched his crotch.
It was all happening inside the city.
And at the edge was desert.

14
Middle East music on the radio: Hebrew love songs,
Arab wails. Carmel Dry Gin
taking me up Zion's hill.
Lights on the stones of the ancient city.

15
Who needs more happiness? People living
on the edge (of pain, of death,
of revelation) need time in the sun,
a lengthening interval between
the sonic boom and the rattled glass.

16
I cannot dissever my happiness from language
or from your body. Light a candle for me
at the false tomb of David, I am of that line.
Let the young scarecrow who might be from 47th Street
say a blessing for me. Sway over the candle's flame
like the old Arab riding toward me on his donkey.
If I forget my happiness, let me be dust.

Jerusalem, here I am going up again.
It is your moon, your labyrinths, your desert
crowding east where the sun waits.

SONG

It was as if she had brought the cooling rain,
the breeze through the curtained window,
the taste of the bourbon,
so that I turned to the street again,
happy in the traffic and the rain.

National Cold Storage Company

1988

HISTORY

1

It was his own scream he heard in the act,
center stage, ego driven, self-expressed.
Her fingers, extravagantly wild.
Dragon Lady. Lurid. Night colors
of deep red, black.

2

You spread the lines, six lines,
on the glass tabletop. This was
our evening at home.
I am not even permitted to call you.
It upsets you, you said, it
leaves you depressed.
Cloth of gold, you sat opposite me,
open and vulnerable, the foreplay
of eyes and speaking tongue.

OBSERVATIONS

1

At Yaddo, 1949,
W. C. Williams tells me
about this guy
who shot himself
while on the phone
to his girl: "You see," says Bill,
"he was a muff-diver."

2

Has there ever been a useful critic?
Longinus, of course, whose text
preserves lines by Sappho.

3
She had his scalp on her belt.
He had her voice in his poems.

4
Studiously third person,
weighted down with family angst,
suddenly in his Education
Henry Adams notices
"the frail wreck of the grasshopper summer."
He has touched his childhood
with his manhood.

TWO CORNELL DEATHS

Because I live I must search these graves.
Coming out of Patchin Place onto 10th Street,
past the iron gate, the figure of Cummings
slouching there, the women ranged
along the street, heads craned
to the barred windows, now silent,
of the Women's House of Detention,
I go to have a drink with Charlie Weir.

He was writing mysteries, working on a novel,
toiling in the wardrobe room of NBC.
In Ithaca he had sometimes missed his classes.
When the train rounded the bend,
hurrying to New York, he flung
his blue books on the tracks, then
marked the grades. For which he was sacked.
Reputed to be a brilliant teacher.

The facts mean nothing in the light of day.
What was the caliber of the weapon?
Partying in Ithaca, thin Jack Sessions
in the corner, another ghost.
He wrote the story of a blind man

who recovered his sight and found
his wife impossibly ugly. She
whom he had loved. What was
the caliber of his weapon, and what other
damage did he do? Last spotted
in a restaurant in the Village.

Pain leaks into this December light.
I take these ghosts with me wherever I go,
asking them, Why now? Why this moment?
Because the liquor is inexhaustible,
the girls will stand at the bar
and smile at the stories, as they used to do.
If you walk by the river, Manhattan
is like a book, the pages turn,
the words march down those pages.

Look back to the lights along the river.
Wait for the dark, wait for the city to come on,
windows and bridges blazing.
Whatever you needed was there, wasn't it?

FROM AN AUTOBIOGRAPHY

I was conceived on the night
of my sister's funeral.
As a replacement, I suspect.
But she was very beautiful,
my mother said, and when I was born
I was quite ugly, with a large bump
on my head, so large the attending doctor first
advised surgery. My grandmother
insisted she could do the job
with the flat of a kitchen knife:
using almost constant pressure.
And so it turned out. My mother,
when she saw me said, Why did God

take away my beautiful child and give me
this ugly baby instead. And she turned away,
not to touch me
for the first few months of my life.
This is family history.
What is unclear is my father's role.
Was the night of my sister's funeral
a suitable time for making love?
Did they both think that?
Or was my father excited by my mother's grief?
Though I honor my mother and father,
I want to ask a few more questions.
When I was very young I heard my mother say
(though she later denied it when I used
the information in a poem) that my father,
blaming her for my sister's death,
did not attend the funeral.
My mother, against his advice,
had taken my sister to visit a sick cousin.
This was 1923. Whooping cough was the killer.
My father has been dead for 16 years,
my mother for two. Among her effects,
I found a large photograph I had never seen before.
In it she is holding my sister, who is
indeed beautiful. My mother is 20 in the picture
and very happy, almost serene,
she whose anxiety is with me still.

COMMENT

Stepin Fetchit—this is from
his obituary in the *Times*—justifying
his life, the eyeball rolling
he had done for his movie pay,
spoke of Bill Cosby and Sidney Poitier:
"I set up thrones for them to come
and sit on." A noble quote, like
"We are, in midmost ground, our own dead kings."

Blackmur's iambic roll to it.
That he, down the long avenue, could
find himself, in purple stuff, leading the way.

AUTOBIOGRAPHY

The clouded sky over Brooklyn
made his meditations shapely.

Fire escapes with pigeons on them.
A leafy street.

Moments when life
tended to make sense.

Earlier, when the kids
were young, taking them to the beach.

Appetite, as in the crow's cry.
Searching the bright shards.

CURTAINS

Equipped with an imagination for disaster,
you never seem to anticipate the real disasters.
They leave you stunned, with no second line
of defense. Then, after days or weeks,
you begin to celebrate them, reciting inwardly
their advantages, how they free up
the imagination for a while. Not that what happened
was exactly falling-down funny. No,
it was more like curtains in the colorful world of death.

LAST THINGS

Is it a failure of my imagination
that I cannot believe in the end of the world.
Or that I believe in it, quietly, as I do in death
but in its own good time. Though, of course,
I understand the weapons are at hand, madmen are loose.
People I loved were concerned, are concerned.
I drift off into the orbit of my own troubles
finding them more familiar, I suppose, though
also more immediately painful. I think
I have made my choice. Others must make theirs.
Nothing can be done to coerce the unwilling
or to safeguard them or us if our dreams
project dragons reeling across a waste of sky.

CYNTHIA

When I take off your red sweatpants,
sliding them over the ass I love,
the fat thighs, and now my hands
are trembling, my tongue is muzzy,
a fire runs under my skin.

Cynthia's red-gold muff caught
the morning light as she strode from my bed,
upright and proud. Her body was
a vehicle for pleasure. It had carried us
into sleep as if we were children,
protected forever from the void and dark.

She slept with him
if at dinner he pleased
her. If he did not, she
did not. She was free
to choose, without
the drags of love.

Every day I wonder about you—
why it is your eyes look so wild
sometimes. Other times, so naked,
so pure-blue naked. Your shields, you say,
speaking of your diaphragm, your contact lenses.
Nevertheless, you think of yourself as being at home
in this world in a way I am not.
I understand it is my myth-making intelligence
gets me in trouble, makes me want to fix you
as earth nourisher, source of comfort,
when it is what is lost and erratic in you
brings you to my bed, beatings against fate
or circumstance, stabbings toward transcendence
that leave us both bruised and happy in ourselves.

To be with her
was to be in a cloud
of sexual joy—hair, eyes,
speech. The merest
flick of her tongue
on a word set off
resonances.

I fell in love with
one of the poisonous tomatoes of America.

Mind-fucking at 3 A.M.
because where are you
and that's where you are.

At the instant of her coming, she makes a throaty sound.
It is back beyond words, low in the throat,
away from the tongue. I never try to translate it,
any more than I would translate sunlight or deep shade.

Before sleep, C in my arms, her back toward me,
puts my right hand on her left breast. If I
could make an amulet of that.

She is beautiful to me
as she wakes from sleep,
sits straight up—
force, energy, and purpose
in her straight spine.

I wonder where her cunt is tonight
and her proud head. She did
make me happy, more than once.
One Sunday morning, light everywhere
in the living room, she on the couch
facing me, garbed in my blue bathrobe,
one breast shapely through the opening
of the robe while I drink my coffee, happy.

The last time
I went down on Cynthia
was the last time
though her petals
in the rose red light

       She said she had taken on seven students the previous
night on her visit upstate, and that all had watched,
masturbating as each colleague performed. One had her
in the missionary position, one took her from behind,
one made her ride on top, one came in her mouth, one
had her lean over a table, one did her on his lap, one fucked
her up the ass. The last to have her, she said, because
he had come six times, had trouble achieving an erection.
After she had told all this to her lover, fiction or fact,
he became the eighth man.

All the questions she asked him
he answered from another life.

He was trying to understand
the nature of the pain.
Maybe when a woman
aborts a child
it is like this: Killing

something in oneself.
Someone else has already done
the killing, yet there
is more left to kill.

She was hidden in his thought
like a tick in a dog's fur.
He could feel the rise with his finger
where her mouth sucked blood.

COMBAT

In the war in which I fought
not all my actions were heroic.
I remember particularly the time
I bargained with God—the plane
seemed to be going down,
smoke filled the cabin—
if he would only get me out alive,
I would . . . What was my promise,
my heartfelt vow? Tears in my eyes,
probably, and trembling. I might
have been speaking to a woman.

ITALY, 1944

That day when we came back from a mission,
in a field beside the tents where we slept
lay a woman and a baby under a blanket.
Beside the blanket was a pile of lira notes.
A line like a chow line snaked through the field.
She was taking them on, one by one,
a squadron of flight crews and ground crews
who could easily get in town whatever they wanted

for a loaf of bread or a pack of cigarettes
but preferred to stand in a muddy field, watching and waiting,
while the blanket humped and the woman earned
whatever it was she had to earn in one day from that war.

A Day's Portion

1994

THESE ARE THE STREETS

1
The upper strand of the Manhattan Bridge
seen from my window
at five of a December evening—
the lights in a graceful arc,
the lit traffic shuttling the Bridge—
is a piece of God's handiwork now
along with the zebra and the bear.

2
I was part of the restless crowd
but sometimes a hand reached
down for me, pulling me up
into rigor, clarity, real space.

3
Remember when the painters were all doing archaic idols?
Things seemed smaller then.
Even mystery was more manageable.
Now it blunders hugely into our lives
like a canvas by Anselm Kiefer.
These are the streets of New York, hung
with letters of white fire on black fire.

CELEBRATIONS

The tremendous
cornices of evening.
Freed from work
with the populace
streaming into subways.
Emerging on Court Street.
Turner's sky, his clouds.
To be lifted out of myself.
Mind's eye, cast down,
now lifted up.

From *A Day's Portion*, 1994　✦　179

Sound carrying the sense
into its own dark home,
furnished with
the gold-plated gods
of Egypt, gathering light,
a shadow sliding on sand,
a bird wheeling in the wastes of sky.
Causeless celebrations.
Terns skipping along the surface
beyond the first line of breakers.
And sometimes in the scatter shine
a ripple of bait fish.
The silk twist
of what you said to me.
Zukofsky at the end of the street
under the light, white spats,
derby and a big cigar.
The gang on Delancey Street—
Irving Berlin and my Uncle Abe
trying out tunes.

QUESTIONS

The idiot sound of someone's stereo
in the apartment below. The bass thudding
like something caught in a trap.
People live in that racket the way I live
with my questions, the things I don't know.
For example, an image of the successful life,
or what is the good, or how can I get
from here to where I want to be, and where is that.

NEW YORK SUMMER

On my block, on an August night,
the air conditioners whir
like wings trying to take off.
The whole city wants to escape this summer darkness,
to head into an Arctic dawn,
cold and clear, to become an impenetrable
ice city, Leningrad in winter
by the banks of the frozen Neva,
the Puerto Ricans covered in fur,
urging their dogs to drink the mineral-clear
vodka, so the soul can make it
through one more jungle day.

MEDITATION ON A BROOKLYN BENCH

I was by myself on the promenade,
facing the massive city. Pleasure craft
cut white trails in the water.
The lady with the lamp dim green
in the dim green afternoon.
A Circle Line boat, looking sprightly,
hurrying upriver, toward the Bridge,
and the old paddle steamer from
the South Street Seaport meandering
past Battery. The kind of day you
needn't take responsibility for, sitting
in the shade, like an elderly citizen,
wondering where it all went—the wife
and kids, the years of work. Covered over
by the waters of the East River. Not a river,
a tidal basin, and the tide coming in now,
full force, dangerous, looking for me.

CITY ETHIC

In New York
at the end of the day
if you are pleased with yourself
and the human condition
and feel no survivor's guilt,
you have added to the darkness.

HOLLYWOOD NOTE

She showed me her office.
She told me she had been fucked
by Francis Ford Coppola
and someone even more famous.

BROOKLYN HEIGHTS

In this corner of the world
live two traditions, four dead poets.
Walt Whitman and Hart Crane, full-voiced
opera on the stereo, American
enterprise swaggering the street.
Louis Zukofsky and George Oppen:
thin Jews, thin Jew music, tessellated
language, ruminative words. All walking
where the ferryboats sparkle.

BROOKLYN NIGHTS

We are like inhabitants
of a southern river town
gathering summer evenings by the water.
A flock of bridges greet us

and the stone hunks of Manhattan.
The power of redemptive love, like
New Jersey red, has gone into the clouds.
Everyone must feel it.

FACT

On the evening of July 3
I saw the Goodyear blimp
for the first time that summer,
over Jersey. Not that my heart leaped up.

LESSONS

1
At Park Place you make out
what the subway conductor is saying
over the crackling speaker:
"This train is going to the Bronx."
Then you understand the world extends
beyond your concerns.
You're getting off at 42nd
but this train is going to the Bronx.

2
That gull on the rocks of the East River,
near the pilings of the Brooklyn Bridge,
has the plastic rim of an empty six-pack
around his neck, his beak just
free enough to pick flotsam
from the water. He seems unconcerned,
adjusted, like the rest of us.

3

The man asked me
for some change for a hot meal.
I walked on, hardening my heart
against myself and against my children
and the whole future of the race.

AUGUST, FROM BROOKLYN

In the sun, walking the Bridge.
A stir of water and shipping
in the windy air. These citizens
seem content with the spectacle.
They pose against the rigging.
They snap each other. Their faces
are bright with a vision of the Narrows.
Their eyes follow a distant ferry.
If they stood at the edge of the
Sangre de Cristo mountains in Colorado
or on the Rainbow Trail, glancing high
to patches of snow, they could not
show more amused wonder than they do now
at the Oz-like minarets and towers of Manhattan.

LOWER EAST SIDE

On Houston Street, walking west,
the moon coming up over Katz's Delicatessen,
we pass a synagogue ancient as Tiberias.
You don't have to be touched
by the hand of God
to pick up on these New York clichés.
We get finished walking the dog
and climb to your Catholic-kitsch apartment
where your Mother of God helps me out of my clothes
and history and the ruined smell of these lives.

LIT CRIT

Street Scene

You are crossing Broadway at 42nd
and you come upon Dante and Virgil
sightseeing, exchanging observations
on the people and the action
as they do in the great poem.
It is winter, and steam from underground
obscures the street. Dante has Virgil
by the arm. You never think
of Dante as a city poet,
but he clearly knows the way.

Crazy Jane Does Yeats

Old he was, limp he was,
I nursed him slowly,
hand and tongue. My finger
in his bunghole. He said,
"Better than Byzantium."

Poe

Entering Poe's
region of novelty and wonder,
where living inhumation
is the order of the day,
I try to escape the drag
of being the subject of this sentence
dutifully following
the participial phrase
when in fact I am not.
Poe is. It is his America
these days, particularly on the screen.
Arthur Gordon Pym,
lost in Antarctica,
the exhalations of his breath
our starry flag.

Composing

The mind falling through space,
looking for a handhold, a foothold.

Country

Crow's insistence that he knows the way.
Possibly he does. Others have said the same:
Satisfy hunger, for whatever, before night.

Romantics

Thinking about why Byron didn't teach Shelley
to swim that summer in Switzerland, ✦
I see why my fellow feeling
for poets goes just so far.

Library

Cynthia got herself off in the stacks
at UCSD. This thought warms me
as I sit by myself in a library at Duke,
remembering her voice and her careful diction
describe how the desire to manipulate
her clit came from the heavy breathing of lit.

Different Schools

In his arena, travesties.
In mine, a death struggle
(I like to think)
with a hallucinatory beast.
A scorched landscape
across which the hero
comes bearing in his hand
the severed head,
still smoking, eyes red,
emitting words that seem
to contain a promise of sleep.
Meanwhile in his arena,
flags, trumpets, cross-dressing,
and a sun god who looks
like the sun.

ON WRITING

1

When the young hood snarls at him,
Sam Spade says, "The cheaper the crook,
the gaudier the patter."
Does this apply to poets?

2

Organize your verse
around a woman—
see Yeats and Dante—
then throw in
the world and death.

3

We file into the chapel
and his verses are read to us in greeting.
Before we file out, his body is wheeled by.
The words of a dead maker prepare to go on trial
through the long seasons of rain and snow.

4

You, lady, leaning down
from the gold bar of heaven,
shine for me over Seventh Avenue,
get me across streets safely,
follow me into dark subways,
remind me of my buried life.

SUNDAY SCHOOL

Walk and be whole, the Bible says,
among the other things it says
about fratricide and filial sacrifice.
Walk and be whole, out of the house.

BIBLE LESSON

When it's time for the Sacrifice
Abraham pays for his stardom
with terror and sweat.
The risk of talking with God.
At some point he could say to you:
Listen, this is what I want you to do
for me next, take your son, your only
son whom you love . . .

GENESIS

He said it is good
and we go out
into it each morning
carrying our shields,
not against chaos—
the midnight terror—
but against all that was
created in orderly fashion
when the lesser light
and the greater light were hung.

AFTER THE FALL

Adam's sentences went into
syntactical overdrive.
Nothing on the planet was safe
from the gray veil of language.
Therefore, God posted the winged sphinxes
and the flashing ever-turning sword.

FOR PAUL CELAN AND PRIMO LEVI

Because the smoke
still drifted through your lives,
because it had not settled—
what would that settling be?
A coming to terms with man's savagery?
God's savagery? The victim
digging deeper into his wound
for the ultimate face?
That would be like saying
we mourn you, when you
have taken all the mourning words
and left us a gesture
of despair. To understand despair
and be comfortable with it—
something you could not do—
is how we live. Sun
drifting through smoke
as I sit on my roof in Brooklyn
with words for the Days of Awe.

TONIGHT

1
I turned on the kitchen light
and saw in the sink what I
took to be a mother roach
and her three young
drinking water from a drop
like deer at a forest pool.

2
When Cheops, our old cat, died,
she climbed into the bathtub
(something never seen before)
to signify going down the drain.

3
Look at it
this way, my son said:
Rabbi Akiba
was unlettered at forty.
Hope for the aging father.

4
This is the angel of death.
When he tells you what he wants
and how you must go about it,
lights out.

LOYALTY

They have been driven insane by history,
my tribe.
They are totally crazy.
Bialik's little Talmudist
and the settler with the gun.
Don't I know firsthand
their self-dramatizations and
their absolute assurance—here in America—
about what constitutes the good life
(my dead mother still telling me from Miami).
My mother, my tribe.
Strung out on wires
in black and white.
God can forsake them, whenever.
Hasn't He?
He has the option.
I don't.

SNAPSHOT

I was listening to a black
clarinetist play Klezmer
at the Knitting Factory on Houston Street
in the bleak December of my 65th year.
Beer was Buber in my head.
My Jewish eyes were brimming.
I shuffled my feet.
I shook my head.

ASSIMILATION

Carl Hubbell, a pitcher for the Giants
when I was a kid, taught me
that what my mother said
about the importance of new clothes and making
a neat impression wasn't true.
He shambled to the mound, his pants
drooped. But he stood there,
fanning the side.
Later, I recognized his type
in Robert Sherwood's play about young Lincoln,
another awkward American
intent on some vision
of the perfect pitch, which my mother,
not born in this country,
still clambering on board,
couldn't get. I knew
it had nothing to do with shined shoes
and slicked-down hair.

NATURAL HISTORY

The dinosaurs, to survive,
became birds. The Jews
of Europe became
smoke. What can you
do as smoke?

JERUSALEM

1
I wonder if Abdullah Shliefer,
my friend and Jewish apostate,
is even now writing
the lost poems of Shabbatai Zevi,
those he composed in
the Sultan's court,
high on hash and oblivion.

2
Dawn seen from
the little balcony
off Shlomo Cohen's
guest room in Jerusalem,
the sun just touching
the mosque; its golden
dome still smoky
with last night's talk.

3
At the end of time
will I be with the other Jews
crowding the narrow entrance
of the El Al gate,
cleared for takeoff
from New York and Tel Aviv.

BRONX ELEGY

That particular Jew, in his community,
observing the Law.
A policeman enshrined within him,
the unlovely way it was put in the eulogy.
Yet the crush of all those people,
the hum of conversation around the plain
pine coffin before the service started
so that the dead man could sleep
as he might in his living room,
nodding off to familiar voices.

A TEL AVIV NOTEBOOK

1
Desultory humping of dogs,
out of boredom.

2
A man at a party in Tel Aviv,
when I brought up the subject
of Genesis, *Bereshit,* because
I felt I was in some way
close to a beginning, began
to spout Latin, the scriptures
in Latin. It seems he owned
a 1504 edition, in the Roman tongue,
and wanted me to know that.
He was glossy with success,
my age, with a young wife,
breasts on display. The rest
of his collection was at home.

3
In the days of Alexander
when the Torah was translated
into Greek, on the island of Pharos,
as a light to the world
(or at least to the Hellenized Jews
who could no longer read Hebrew),
the world was plunged into darkness
for three days,
according to the Rabbis,
who knew what followed:
the fall of Rome,
you, me and Irving Berlin.

4
Hebrew, once a language of dislocations and disasters,
the major disaster a meeting
of a people with God,
cheerfully blends with the cooing of doves
in the Galilee. It is a speech
of infants, or for the old
to speak to the young. It is
only when lovers use it
that history muscles in.

5
When he comes
what will he bring?

Happiness, I'm sure
for the used and hungry.

Neediness for the rich,
to let them taste the world.

A crying without end
for the unjustly dead.

He will raise them all
according to his word.

Some of them will be a sight
searching for their limbs.

Will he still the traffic
in the city streets

as all look up to find
the final messenger?

When he comes
what will he bring?

6
If it is true, as Rabbi Kook asserts,
that the Holocaust was God's
last-ditch effort to remind Jews
of the fundamental facts of life,
the realization of which
brought Israel into being,
we are back in a comfortable world.

7
"Your people of Israel
who are in
the four winds of heaven."

AUBADE

As you watch from the bed,
the women rise in their glory
to go to the john. They are
suddenly full-length, dazzling,
the crown of their hair
in the morning light. Bare to their feet
on the wooden floor, moving
as if through a green field,
they bring blue sky into the room
to frame them where they stand
in the immutable space of their being.

From *A Day's Portion,* 1994   ❖   195

HIS AGE

1

An afternoon of it
left him "blissed-out,"
he told the woman,
realizing in his sixties
he had learned the word
in the Sixties. To the woman
it was a shining
ancient coin.

2

This vapid light
in which it is necessary
to work, to make bread,
to become a believer in
the true unfathomable light.

3

Whom do you live with?
I was lost in action.
My plane went down.
They couldn't find me
in the jungle. The years
have grown over me.

4

"The god who loosens the limbs,
and damages the mind,"
in Hesiod's Englished words,
has figured in my lines
too often: Eros, destroyer
of meaning and creator of song.

5

I asked her what she was thinking.
She said there was nothing on her screen.

TABLE SCENE

When a woman says to you,
explaining some inexplicable action,
"That is the way I am,"
you imagine her peering into
a rich garden, a small park
really, filled with scent and
romantic statuary. A soft wind
sweeps through it, and from time to time
plangent sounds issue from the park
touched by the soft wind. You too
sit in wonder at the way she is.

HISTORY

I can remember when I was in the grip of passion.
I can't simulate, by will, the emotion
but I can remember the signs, the irrational actions
that drove my life off the track, assuming there was
a track, and that still deal their consequences,
though whatever god inhabited me then has long
forgotten what I look like and my name.

THE ENCOUNTER

As she came, she began to cry.
Later, in the middle of the night,
not touching you, she said I love you.
It wasn't as if she had thought to herself,
I'll say the three little words.
It was more like the words
were a delayed part of the cry of her coming
and were being shown to you furtively,
and against her will.

POLITICS

"I'm on the bloody rag,"
she said. Flag
of my allegiance.

PLEASURE

I begin again, having no alternative
unless it be to hear others speak.
But what would they say?
Reach in, she said,
and get some juice.
That was happiness.
Her absence puts me in mind
of who I am. Her absence
and her presence, both.
That figure, seen through
the rain-spattered window
approaching on Hicks Street,
at a distance. Behind it a red light,
behind that a green.
Beyond, the lights of two bridges.
And the City, variform, insensate,
always in my sight.
The night hum, as if from her voice,
her hair. The precise words
with which she says,
when she pleases, what pleases her.
Pleasure, in the sense
of remembered pleasure.
The striking of one word, and then another.
Because she gave me
a dictionary of music
to answer the questions
she could not answer.

ANOTHER STORY

The whole drift of the world disturbs her:
technology out of hand, pride of work
lost. She tells him all this and keeps
telling him this, and what she is telling him is
that she doesn't see what she loves before her.

BELIEF SYSTEMS

What it comes down to,
though you could choke
on the phrase, is a reverence for life.

Include in that
C at the edge of the bed in the morning,
the cleft of her ass as she
bends to find her socks.

EDUCATION

When a woman takes off her clothes
a man's education begins.
She was wearing biker's panties,
black and slightly padded,
with an inscription on the back:
"A Classic Bitch."

A STORY

He was married.
She wanted him in his own space.
She wanted him motivated. "Be happy,"
she said, "you love me." She helped him

buy suits and overcoats and spend money
lovingly on himself. She set him going
like one of those toy tops, lights on,
music humming, and watched him into the dark.

FANCY

The kinds of excitement—
jealousy, rage or love—
lurking in his thought that night
presumed the human.
He wanted out of that.
It was an inhuman time.

He saw the
water towers
of Manhattan as African
warriors guarding the roofs.

Fancy, or the aggregative power,
as Coleridge said, brings together
images dissimilar in the main
by some one point or more of likeness.

Nude, she sat on the edge of the bed.
They were preparing to go out.
Her breasts fell forward
into her black lace brassiere.

HOW IT ENDED

1
In the name of love
she sent me to her accountant
who confirmed I was a loser.

2
Because I'm drinking
I think I'm writing
but actually
I'm only drinking.

3
The muse never lets you off the hook.
Tired and sodden, depressed,
whatever, you have to get it up
for her or taste the acid of defeat.

WHEN THE SPIRIT

When the spirit begins to shut down,
it is real enough. No abstract entity then.
No useful fiction. You can hear it
banging down the window, saying
this shop is closed. And you know
it could mean forever. Where will your
legs carry you then, and of what
use to you your eyes?

BEFORE SLEEP

He faced a man who was writing,
who seemed serious in his writing,
whose seriousness rebuked him
for both the irresponsibility with which he wrote
and the irresponsibility with which he lived.
It was better to turn out the light and forget the man.

ON MY PORTRAIT BY ROSE GRAUBART

I never thought
my mouth was lost
in such darkness,
such desperate darkness,
smeared in ashes
almost a whole face full.
Or is it the asshole of the world
I'm talking my way through.
To the light, Rose,
to the light!

OCEAN DAWN

Sun rising out of the sea
in old Miltonic splendor.
Light raging to cover space.
My own clot of darkness
searched out on the still beach.

THE TEXT

The way the names cluster
in the text, giving
a nominative reality to the world.
All of it, a book of naming.
The sun, adrift with all the planets,
on a journey that is not a journey
since it has no direction.
Aimless drift, while
on this oblate sphere
we build the nominative towers.
I wanted to believe in my life
so fiercely, like a boy
masturbating himself into a dream.

FOR CHARLES REZNIKOFF

Evening star over Jersey
making it through the smog.
A black tug rounding Battery.
I put these down in my ledger,
Charles, walking and watching,
which is the way we serve.

I agree, Charles, to read and write
by daylight is a great pleasure. So
I sit by my window
this Saturday morning intent
on putting words to the page,
not as carefully as you placed them there—
I haven't the patience or the art—
but in my quick time, in my slapdash
fashion, to celebrate the morning light
and to say that to arrive at 62 years,
which I will do next Monday,
and still to take pleasure
in writing, marks me as a lucky man.
And to have known you and your
great sweetness for so many years
of your life, and in memory still,
makes me doubly lucky. There is
such good company at the common table.
We sit there, each with the work in his hands.

SAROYAN

A few days before Saroyan died
he called Associated Press
from his hospital bed in San Francisco
and said: "I know everyone dies
but I always thought an exception
would be made in my case.
Now what?" There was no answer

to that question. Saroyan's voice
was stentorian, up-volume,
partly because he was hard of hearing.
The question, like a frail boat, put out to sea.

A DAY

The morning begins with contention.
It is a day I meant to sanctify,
all by myself, with words of my choosing.
And now you have scribbled over it
the facts of our life.

It sounds like realism.
But look—
it is melodrama.

TRANQUILITY

His liver-spotted hand on hers.

1943

Because we had to shoot at a moving target
from a moving target, they placed us
on flat-bed trucks and sent us around
a circular track, much like a race course.
At stations along the way, clay pigeons
were released—our moving targets. And we,
moving too, with rifles in our arms,
fired at those birds, learning to lead them
into the obliterating future, high over Germany.
That was gunnery school. Yuma, Arizona,
where the tanks crawled a desert

that stretched from Marrakech to Sicily.
I travel back those forty years to salute
the imperial legions, boys and their machines.

BLOWING SMOKE

These beautiful cigars,
De Nobili, with the colors of Italy
on the package, though
the tobacco is the finest
from Kentucky and Tennessee,
please my taste and my wallet:
90 cents for five. I smoke
them with my bourbon,
remembering the lights
of Covington and Hall, towns
I viewed from a B-17
on night training flights over Tennessee
during the war. I bought my
setups at the Peabody Hotel
in Memphis. It was
the start of a beautiful life.

IGGY

The exercises I do each morning
before I brush my teeth
I learned in the Air Force,
in Miami Beach, during basic training
from a young man—we were all young men—
named Iggy. He had volunteered
to lead our squad in exercise each morning
because that is what he had done in the Catskills
summers to earn his rent, putting
squads of women through their paces
before the ingestion of the heavy breakfast.

And so each morning, I memorialize
those women, sweating in the mountain sun—
dead now, I suppose—and Iggy,
and myself, young and full of hope.

SELF-PORTRAIT

He was favored by the gods
in all his endeavors.
They made sure he never
snuggled into safe harbors.
All his reports of the world
were written on the run
and from a troubled spirit,
as if he were an Odysseus who could
never get home to bore the company
with smug tales of his performance.

THE BOAST

Never using a stuntman,
I went through this life myself.

YEARS AGO

Rain is in the air, or
falling so gently
it seems part of the air.
My son glides in, leans
his bike beside the porch,
waiting it out. He objects
to my singing "April Showers"
when it's almost August.
I stop singing

and we listen to the quiet.
When the rain stops
he moves off into the sand
beside the house
to build something with a long
story attached, which he tells
himself as he goes along,
handful by handful.

SHOPPERS

Now I'm the age of the retirees
in Hollywood, Florida, in the Galahad South,
where my parents lived. The talk
around the pool was often of money saved,
the great bargains of the day. The last days
of the shoppers. In my Key Food in Brooklyn
the manager calls over the speaker: Shoppers!
How many shaves do you get to a blade
was much discussed among the men. Shoppers,
as we head into the sunset what is it
we wish we had purchased with our lives?

A DAY'S PORTION

1
At 3 A.M.
I had my happiness back.
I rose to meet it, knowing
how far it must have traveled.

2
A day's portion every day,
gather it is the commandment.
Gather what, I ask,
my hands full of trouble.

3
There are the ecstatic endings
and there are the endings that make sense.

THE DEFENSE

1
Will I ever again see
the white implacable Aphrodite?
Maybe on the subway or in the street.

2
And drove the iron tears down Priam's cheek.
Achilles, speaking of his own loss, did that.
White shipping making white wakes on the beaten-metal bay
this clear June day. I sit across from Battery,
the green of its triple arches rising from the water
like the Venice of my imagination.
"It's a universal law," someone says in passing.
And older voice, rich in surety.
I don't look up, bent over my writing pad,
studying the chaos of my life.

3
Unable to find a cure for death or defense against age,
men remember gigantic actions leading to death,
talk about them, create them again in vividness
as Homer created Troy and its feast for birds.

FROM

Selected Poems

1997

WHAT IT FEELS LIKE

The first night out of Eden
or rather the first morning
after the first night out is
what it always feels like.

I can have a bagel and coffee
but only after I arrive at work.
Until then the despair is too great.
It was different when I woke with you
and prayed to the white curve of your back
and cradled it like the ark of the covenant.

IN TIBERIAS

Rabbi Akiba
measured the distances
of angels, archangels and principalities
from the throne of God.
It was probably on an August
afternoon like this one,
his beard tangled in calculations,
the noise outside his window —
an old man beating his donkey—
making him aware than angelology
is a refuge like any other.

EPITAPH

Death floats my boat.

PRAGUE

The Gothic half-light
in which moulder
the stones of the Jewish cemetery,
a tumbled mass of stones
crowded on each other
like the cadavers in the camps,
so that you keep sliding out
of one picture into the other.

"The world is a narrow bridge,"
said Rabbi Nachman,
"the important thing
is not to be afraid."

1949

Memories of Ted Roethke at Yaddo.
He slept beside an inscribed picture of "Dylie"—
as if they were lovers—
when I came to wake him after my lunch,
and he would rise, vomit,
mix a pitcher of martinis and we
headed for the tennis court.

Or standing hugely tall in his white suit
at a bar near the track in Saratoga,
he discussed the rival gangs—the
Jarrell gang, for example—
and what we might do to wipe them out.
Or he talked about knocking over a bank
and earning a fellowship. Tall, broody,
drink in hand, king of the rackets.

Or dragging a carton of poetry books
onto the lawn, along with a bottle
of wine kept chilled in the hall refrigerator,

he read for a while, then tried to write.
He asked me once for the lines in Wordsworth
describing a boy racing over a field.

Or reaching back, he told me how
John Crowe Ransom had rejected
"My Papa's Waltz" when it was
submitted to him at the *Kenyon Review*.
And Roethke's eyes filled with tears—
his poem already anthology-famous but the wound
open still. The Garden Master but
tendril-tender all his short life.

CHOICES

He contemplated the bad poetry
he could have written had he
retired to Florida, following
the path his parents had blazed.
He could have described the gulls
winging it over the parking lot,
the thin strip of sand threading the coast
between the poured concrete and the sea.
Friday night bingo and the trailer camps.
Pelicans patrolling the blue-green water.
And the sunsets—drink in hand
standing on the tiny balcony
with the whole fantastic opera
played out in living color.
Or maybe on a party boat out of Haulover,
the Cuban lady of his adolescent dreams,
the lady in red shorts and cap,
could have hooked him hard,
blown him to one last good time,
beached him moneyless and staggering,
with visions in his head and songs to sing.

HART

His mind had been habituated
to the Vast, living in Brooklyn,
across from the white buildings.

He came upon the heart's
big ecstasy one night
on the IRT

because what else is there
but death.

GENERATIONS

In the meridian heat
watching the hummingbird's
air-borne dance, not far
from the blue harp of Kinneret
tilting to my sight
like the tables of the law,
in Galilee, in Jesus country,
near the diner marked "Loaves and Fishes"
from which I can see
myself in the maze of New York,
following my father's ghost, maybe
with less sense than he
of the promised land.

THE TICKET

The poet saw the moon dimglimmering
through the dewy windowpane.
It was a 19th-century moon, soft as moths.
And he was on laudanum or opium.
Only yesterday when I asked her on the phone

why she sounded so happy, she replied:
"I'm on psychopharmaceuticals and in the country."
Ah, that's the ticket.

ITALY, 1996

This Italian earth is special to me
because I was here in a war
when I was young and immortal.
I remember the cypresses in the early morning light
on the road to the airfield
before the sky filled with toiling planes
massing high over Italy for the perilous
crossing to Germany. I remember
on the way back from the target toasting
my frozen cheese sandwich—frozen by the high altitude—
on the electrically-heated casing of my fifty-caliber
machine gun. I remember the taste of life.

TRAVELING THROUGH IRELAND

I
Sitting beside a sign
pointing to Cork and Limerick
or in Irish *Corcaigh*
and *Luimneach,*
I am persuaded again
of my foreignness in this world,
and that none of the signs I read
points to happiness. And
many I can't make out.
Though this world is the only world
it is composed of infinite worlds.
In one of them, I take
my rightful place.

2
On the streets of Donegal
little Irish women
chirping like sparrows
pass tall Viking beauties
astride in black leather.

3
The young woman at the desk
of the Great Southern Hotel in Sligo
when she heard I was returning
to New York, said appreciatively:
"Ah, the Big Smoke itself."

4
"It's a long way to Tipperary"
sung at closing time
in a pub in Tipperary
by all assembled—
sorrowfully, joyfully—
explained my life.

5
"Venus could no longer
bear to hear him grieve."
These words, so lovely in Virgil,
I put beside Austin Clarke's
"Nothing I want to do
can make her frown."

6
No horseman will pass by my stone.
If I am to be remembered, let it be
by a young woman on the IRT
getting off at Borough Hall.

FROM

*How Charlie Shavers Died
and Other Poems*

2001

BROOKLYN SNAPS

1
Another gaudy spring in Brooklyn's Botanic Garden.
Under the heavy-laden cherry trees
the scattered families sit, so
many Japanese among them, I think
the trees bend low to catch the talk.

2
The sky itself is a painterly blessing,
a pale wash of blue
with delicate white clouds.
So is the red brick of the low houses.

3
Blessings on the traffic cop who says
"Move your vehicle, sir" to her double-
parked black brother. How the ancient
words ring out on the Brooklyn street.

4
Watching the perps and the cops and the lawyers
on Court Street enter the Supreme Court, State of New York.
Maybe the ugliest building in the borough,
massive concrete bunker with slits for windows,
uglier than the jail on Atlantic Avenue,
only a few blocks south.
Stalin would have loved it.
Still, the juries I've sat on there
have delivered justice. And the open square
leading to it catches the December sun
brilliantly in the morning,
gilding the green benches—if you have
the time and money to enjoy it.

5
A black queen
approaches my car
at the corner of Atlantic and Henry.

"I need $100,000
to help me pick up
the pieces of my life."
A shrug, moves off.

6
A hot haze envelops the city.
Even the buildings seem worn out,
their windows sag. On a bench
in Fulton Ferry Park
an elderly gent sits, killing time.
Yesterday he was young and hopeful.
Tomorrow he might be dead.
In the meantime, he looks at the East River.

7
All his life, he sat on a roof in Brooklyn
as on the deck of an ocean liner. He thinks,
though his voyage was brief, it was sweet.

8
They lift the Chinese delivery boy
from his shattered bicycle.
The Vietnamese taxi driver
stands in the rain, sucking
on a cigarette. White cops
take it all down.

9
A very trim green-and-white
Circle Line boat passing under
the Brooklyn Bridge. It's nice
to see the multitude on board
enjoying the sun and scenery.
Manhattan is my favorite island,
seen from this shore. These days
when I see it in sparkling sun
I think of the poems of Schuyler and O'Hara
as I used to think of Reznikoff and Crane.
Yesterday I saw a man land

a two-pound striper on the pier near
the Bridge. A noble fish. But the fisherman,
speaking in an accent I couldn't place,
told me the Russians were killing all
the fish, big and small. They take
babies, he complained. I figured he meant
off Brighton Beach, not Vladivostok.
Dandelions and lilacs are out in Fulton Ferry Park.

NEW YORK NOTES

1
Caught on a side street
in heavy traffic, I said
to the cabbie, I should
have walked. He replied,
I should have been a doctor.

2
When can I get on the 11:33
I ask the guy in the information booth
at the Atlantic Avenue Station.
When they open the doors, he says.
I am home among my people.

THREE FLIGHTS DOWN THE STAIRS

Three flights down the stairs,
south one block to Houston,
cross the street and maybe a half-block
west to Russ & Daughters.
Take a number—why is that woman
buying all that sturgeon?—for black
Russian bread, 3 smoked fish, farmer
cheese (the bulk kind) and nova.
Retrace the route, up the stairs,

and she's just getting out of the tub
right by the kitchen sink, pink
thighs slowly rising so you can get
the whole flavor of it, water
streaming from the red muff thick
as bread. That was Sunday.

MANHATTAN IN SUMMER

The drier whacking away, next to the refrigerator
in the tumbled together kitchen. You lie
on the bed in your nightgown.
It is this tropical island, Manhattan in summer.
The Puerto Ricans, carrying their music and forlorn star,
have left for the barrios. At Victor's Café,
the green sauce is so splendid
we carry some back to the apartment.
When you leave for your other island, your
New England white steeple and lobster pot town,
I will remain with my cigars and cerveza,
the streets sinking under my feet, the brilliant taxis,
sun fierce on the stones of the Museum.

MOVIE LIFE

"The future ain't
what it used to be"
Robert De Niro says
in *Johnny Angel*.

When my son Dan was born
I sat in a car
outside Columbia Presbyterian,
in a July dawn, weeping
copiously, as light began
to fill the streets and
avenues of my city.

BROOKLYN PROMENADE

There they are
the water-hugging giants of Manhattan
breathing the dun-colored air of morning.
Silent, mysterious
seen through a white scrim of fog.

Directly beneath me, commuter traffic of the Brooklyn-Queens
    Expressway.
Across that, on the Brooklyn docks
one lone forklift tractor, loaded with steel rods,
jockeying back and forth
before the Strober Bros. Building Supply depot.
Across the water, dimly descried,
nested in the green arches of Battery,
a perky yellow Staten Island Ferry.

But the buildings pulsing in their various shades of white
and now, as the fog thins slowly,
a pale dusty blue, out of Giotto,
seems to descend behind them.

These mighty presences at the end of Manhattan Island,
fronting the East River that is not a river
but a tidal strait carrying
the North Atlantic to our very doorstep.

These monuments that dominate our day
as if they had been fixed there forever
though they are in flux as the waters are in flux.

They stand before us
like tribal gods meting out success and unsuccess,
all that we have to lift our eyes to.

FAMILY

The thickness of things I felt strongly,
sitting in the sun, in a public place,
people strolling, voices in different languages,
as if life were a canvas—
but one would have to know the drama
and recognize among all the clumsy figuration
who is caught in the vectoring lines.
A pigeon bathing
in a puddle on the roof of a warehouse
abutting the Brooklyn waterfront, looking in its preening
like a blue heron eastward down the island,
in Gardiner's Bay, among the blues of summer.
But this is November, in Brooklyn, and I look
to the smaller island where my father and mother,
each in turn, came to the New World.
Voices across the bay, my grandmother's Yiddish
talking to the Yiddish of her green-boxed radio.
Is that the drama—bewildering change and nostalgia?
Enter the New World, mother and father.
Sit on the bench with me, overlooking Pier 3 of the Brooklyn
Port Authority Piers. Try to make sense of it with me,
and with your other son, who sits by the dark Kinneret.
The harp of David and the harp of the Brooklyn Bridge.

WAR STORIES

1

My father read the World Telegram & Sun.
Sometimes he agreed with Westbrook Pegler.
But he never brought home a Hearst paper
except for the Sunday Journal American
because I was a kid and needed the colored comics—
Maggie and Jiggs, Popeye and Dick Tracy.
All those strips I was to see again in high school
in their porno resurrection, strips
in which even Dagwood had a big erection.
I listened to radio serials every afternoon
from five to six: Buck Rogers in the 25th Century,
Jack Armstrong, the All American Boy.
Each one had a special anthem. Later,
in Sioux Falls, South Dakota, at an army base,
I heard them all again. We were in training
as radio gunners in heavy bombers. It was
midwinter and my group was on the midnight shift,
getting up and marching to class in frigid Dakota dark.
The commanding officer issued a directive:
We weren't singing when we marched as Air Force
    men should—
"Into the air Army Air Force / Into the air pilots true,"—
So from now on sing! The night the directive was read out,
I was marching in the middle of a squad
when suddenly, all around me, everyone
began to sing: "Who's that little chatterbox,
the one with pretty auburn locks. Who
can it be? It's Little Orphan Annie."
And so on through all the songs of all
the serials of my childhood.

2

These are a conquered people,
said the British sergeant,
putting his hand on my shoulder
at the bar in Foggia, Italy—
this is 1944. He was instructing

me on why I should not tip
the Italian barmaid, as I was doing.
A conquered people. I liked the phrase
because it had the ring of history,
suggested dynasty policy, put
the British empire with the Roman
down the long reach of time.
But in the real world it made
no sense. How did it apply
to the Italian kids who came
to my tent each morning to trade
eggs for cigarettes. Or to the old
Italian lady in town who was teaching
me the language. Or to the girl
in the Air Force rest camp on Capri
I fell in love with Christmas week.
They were hardly a people, much less
conquered. They were living
as I lived, on the bare edge of existence,
hoping to survive the interminable war.
But high above their cities
on my way to Germany to kill the enemy
I was part of that sergeant's fictive world,
part of the bloody story of our century.

3
We were approaching Berlin
at 23,000 feet, our usual
altitude for bombing. P38s
looking like flying catamarans,
had accompanied us most of the way—
little friend, little friend—from Italy.
Now, nearing the target, we had P51s.
We knew that when their auxiliary fuel tanks
were jettisoned from their underbellies
and came floating down like silver baubles,
a sky full of them,
enemy fighters would shortly show.
A clear blue light flooded my cabin.
Through my window and hatch

I could see what looked like miles
of Flying Fortresses, the big-assed birds
in their tight formations. Blue all around them,
followed by white contrails. Later,
colored tracers would connect bomber
to enemy fighter, and then the black flak
would spread in the sky, a deadly fungus.
Planes would blossom into flame
in that bewildering sky.
How to believe all that happened
as in a movie, a TV drama, or some other life.

1998

These shards of our lapsed rhetoric,
what a generation meant to say,
speak in me still. A flame guttering.
That the slashed landscape, the railroad
yards, the crumbled snow-strewn depots
of a vanquished Europe, all their dying gods,
flame, flare up, add to the smoke
of sacrifice. Millennial stars,
pools of light, sucking the last meaning
from the tremendous century.
The writers, hunkering down like monks
in their stone outcroppings
over the clear blue slate, catching
visions of the dystopian dawn.

HISTORY

I have lived three-quarters of a century.
I remember the man bringing ice
into the kitchen for the ice box.
He came down the narrow alley
that led to the back of the house.

From *How Charlie Shavers Died and Other Poems*, 2001 ❧ 227

He used tongs to lift the ice.
Our first car was a Nash.
From our window on Riverside Drive
I saw them building the George Washington Bridge.
When you had ice cream at home
your mother had to make it.
Cases of Dr. Brown's Cel-Ray Tonic and Cream Soda.
I kissed my cousin Muriel under the piano.

HOW CHARLIE SHAVERS DIED

He had a gig
but he was hurting.
His doctor said, play the date,
then check into the hospital.
That night, when the party ended
and the band packed up,
Charlie started to give stuff away—
his watch, his rings—to the women
in the room. Then
he circled the room with his horn
playing: "For all I know we may never meet again."
At this point, the man who was telling the story
in the locker room at the Manhattan Plaza gym
and who had sung the line slowly, with
a pause between each word, began to cry.

6/20/97

It's Friday night and I've just had
another helping of Ben & Jerry's coffee
fudge frozen yogurt because I saw
David Ignatow at Columbia Presbyterian,
8th floor, Milstein, room 426, after a quick
ride on the skip 9, the one that does
every other stop, and David, who is

recovering from a stroke, doesn't look
too good, a transparent mask over
his face, feeding him oxygen, whiffs of
steam eddying from it, or maybe con-
trails because David is going very fast,
talking to himself and jerking his body
violently. On the other hand, the view
from his window is splendid, the
lordly Hudson cloaked in late afternoon
sun. I say to the nurse, his color is good,
and she says, that's because we're giving
him blood, pointing to the tubing. Count
Dracula was right, she says, it
makes you look good.
But it's not for real.

AT THE TOMB OF THE POET RACHEL

The silence in the water
and above the water.
The stones like sheep
on the steep hillside, and the
presence of the dead.
To be engaged
in this archaic act
of creating images
that reflect the world
allies me with the dead,
who believed in a reflected world.
You, Rachel, are remembered.
This stone, placed beside the others,
tells you so. The wild
trajectory of a life that
brought you here doesn't matter.
It brought you here, and will
bring others from your pages
to this place, where the road

From *How Charlie Shavers Died and Other Poems*, 2001 ✦ 229

bends to Tiberias
and the ancient world in which
we both live consoles us both.

OPPEN

The muffled sea, until you're at the margin.
Fog up and down the beach. Space obliterated,
the way it must have been for George—
by Alzheimer's—when we walked from
Polk Street where he lived the few blocks
to the San Francisco waterfront, and he
didn't know whether he was in China
or at sea. At sea, I guess, is what it comes down to,
though for most of his life, at sea
meant at home to him. He crafted
the boats in which he rode out the storms.
Needle's eye was close to where he lived.
Then to end that way—compass lost—
who knew the materials, built the rough deck.

HOMAGE TO GEORGE OPPEN

Brooklyn/San Francisco

In that small apartment,
tenement rooms really,
on the other side of Atlantic Avenue,
windows braced with clear plastic
against the wind off the East River.
The words slow, the jumps between the words,
as in the poetry.

"We walk.   We walked up Tamalpais—
the final peak, which is almost
a steeple.   Wonderful   So high
the ocean curved I thought
and pieces of fog went below us.

Occurrence—events   the heavy events—
and down or someplace to the toys
of everyday, small self-interest,
the wings of the wasp.

I think of you reading
the three old Jews who look down.
Well—the three old Jews including Freud
look down, and cluck their tongues,
they always did, they've always been there,
I've heard them clucking—they sure
clucked over me as a G.I., and
they're clucking now
like crickets in a summer evening.

I think the new poems are good
sparse but they move
and yet I wanted them to move elsewhere
Toward greater self-satisfaction?
I guess that's it. Greater complacency.
Drift and drift and drift; the image
everywhere is the sea and its horizon.
Everywhere in my mind too

For all my metaphors of the sea,
they think our feet ain't wet in moments
of anger they suspect
we aren't drowning
                    and they're wrong,
they're wrong, but I see the point
Brilliant and beautiful young people

There comes to me
a variation of that parable
about the note found outside an orphan asylum,
adjusted to the poet:
'To Whoever Understands This: I love you.'

However: the walks! And just places
cafés stores I think we haven't
felt such excitement together
since we were first in Paris
on the great venture"

Note: The words within the quotation marks were selected from letters
George Oppen sent to me.

EAST HAMPTON READING

John Hall Wheelock at eighty stood up, book closed,
and said his poems. They were written in his head
and were in his head still, keeping the sea wind
and the long sunlit beach where he walked and composed
his lines of a gone world, borne now
by the sea wind, scattered on the sunlit beach.

JOHN CLARE

"Joy's manna from its wings doth fall and lie."
Sullen sweepings of my desolate street
bring me back to Clare's bright musings,
country mornings, though my vista isn't
easily put aside—the silent stone
barricades of Manhattan and the water
they miraculously ride. Not that one
needs to deride cities, spawn of Cain,
and in our day the very Babylons on which

a judgment sits—mark the brow of any walker.
Heavenly Clare, to sweeten his asylum mornings,
conjured awhile with poetry. It was
on the wane, he said. So was joy's manna.

FOR ARMAND AND DAVID

When we were young
and our children were young—
the water was such a mystery,
the sky so blue. Everything
breathed promise. The language
would blaze forth,
did blaze forth.

I see the same sights
bleared now. Words
broken into stoney syllables,
blackened in remembrance.

To the rich vacationers
our lives meant nothing.
We kept investing them with meaning
until the enterprise broke us.

This monody
will not wake even the anthologists
who count us
among their small change.

SMALL COMMENTARIES

I
If passion is the transport
and commotion of the soul,
as Longinus says and sets

order at defiance, let the sea
off Montauk in December
speak for me.

2
Donne piles death upon death—
the death of corruption and putrefaction
and vermiculation and dispersion—
because these are all entrances
to eternal life, and so glorifying
and intoxicating (see Dylan
Thomas' "Deaths and Entrances").
But we, denied that key,
see in the dust our last extremity.

3
Who first recognizes Odysseus?
Argos, his dog, after twenty years.
I had forgotten this. Argos, also in his old age,
neglected by all, lies in shit but
at the sound of his master's voice
pricks up his ears, thumps his tail and dies.
Dies happy or at least intact. Rare in Homer.

4
The most lovely thing,
wrote Sappho, pulling from the air
chariots and marching men.
A small trembling begins
throughout her entire body.
Hand dangling.
Cheeks wet with tears.

5
Shakespeare had known,
with a creative intimacy,
Lear, Coriolanus, Macbeth,
Hamlet and I could go on.
Could he then, in his last years,
know himself, or find

that knowledge interesting? Ego-less,
he must have drifted out
among the stars of his devising.

6
Looking for the daily poetry fix
so that he can justify his life.
Not exactly service in a great cause.
Pretty bourgeois when you think of it,
though the need to justify
suggests awareness of the chaos
that blooms inside him and around him
and is fast replacing life.

7
The unreliable narrator of these poems
before he writes
always looks into his heart.

IN THE '50s

There was Jean Garrigue,
the courageous poet, leading
a poet's life on Jones Street.
But maybe a bit antique, considering,
looking back at her
hard gem-like flame.
The thin black ribbon
around her neck was art's wound,
though it didn't stop her
from balling men and women,
including tender Dylan,
who poisoned her style.
Her building in a rose-red light,
the Village tenements
we thought were Paris.

WORKING DAYS

The bar at Schrafft's, corner of Broadway and 43rd,
served the best martinis in mid-Manhattan.
We lunched there often, on three martinis each.
Charlie Palmer, Barney Lefferts and Sherwin Smith.
I was a guest in their Wasp heaven.
They might have chosen a better Jew to chronicle them.
But they had their own phrases. I admired them because
their hatred of what they did for a living was pure.
Newspaper men working for an editor so dense, he would
remark of any sentence that contained a subordinate
clause: "This is something for the Partisan Review."

GREENWICH VILLAGE, 1999

On Grove Street
we talked about writing
in a room jammed with bodies,
but now no smoke. Everything
else was the same, including
my belief that it would never end.
Ken said to Roberta
that because they lived in rent-
stabilized flats, they had
the luxury of writing
all hours of the day and night
and that, so enabled,
they constituted the real
academy of arts and letters.
Outside, the indifferent light
lit up the small street.

AMERICAN POET

Your images come to you like the lost buffalo.
In the sundown of your fancy, in the slanted town,
two men face each other in the street.

After the war, we all lived in a ruined city.
I wore my black tie every day to class.

The night they come calling for you
they don't explain anything. They kick
you around a little, then they reach in
and stop the heart. It's yours
but you can't use it anymore.
They don't explain anything. They
don't have to explain anything.

PLACES

The Pazzi Chapel in Florence
and the Mosque of the Golden Dome
in Jerusalem and Cynthia's cunt
have been the loci of my strongest
aesthetic experiences—overwhelming
solitude and an unearthly light.

CAPE ANN

A bee working over the roses
abutting the white porch
where I sit shaded,
two gazebos before me, beyond
them the soul-immersing sea.
In my dream last night
Robert Lowell came to me
weeping great tears. He

sat across from me, his
body hunched. Someone had passed
bitter judgment on his work
and I, who hardly knew him
in life, had to comfort him
in death, while my own wreckage,
sun-struck, gleamed in the shallows.

ABRAHAM'S PATH

She thought he got his sexual energy from the Kabbalah,
though it was more like a freight train running over her
every night about twelve, runic images of the countryside
floating in her head—a lone fox, hunched in the field,
shining its lamps to the moon—the freight cars rattling
and the long despairing declining note at the end.
He thought she had her orgasms in American.
They were in a speakeasy in New York in the 1920s.
"Hello Suckers" said Texas Guinan, and the floorshow began.

PART OF AN INFINITE SERIES

She raises her nightgown
over her head
like the beginning of a Greek trilogy

She raises her nightgown
over her head
like the Opening of the West

She raises her nightgown
over her head
like a shout in the East Village

She raises her nightgown
over her head
like doves rushing from a dovecote

She raises her nightgown
over her head
like the whirr of low-flying geese

She raises her nightgown
over her head
like a gage to be slammed down

She raises her nightgown
over her head
like the banners of the barbarians

She raises her nightgown
over her head
like a lioness's first stride toward a gazelle

She raises her nightgown
over her head
like God saying, Let there be light

She raises her nightgown
over her head
like a hand writing, In the beginning

She raises her nightgown
over her head
like a traffic cop in Rome stopping traffic

She raises her nightgown
over her head
like a rose reaching ultimate redness

She raises her nightgown
over her head
like Handel's Hallelujah chorus

She raises her nightgown
over her head
like manna descending on the people

FOR GALEN & AFTER O'HARA

I did not take my walk today.
I forgot to eat my clove of garlic
which only two days ago
I made part of my daily regimen.
But I did spend most of the morning
in bed with you making love
while the bright March sun,
a true harbinger of spring,
blazed on the shy head-dropping
snow drop flowers and on
the few scattered clumps of snow.
And later at Two Mile Hollow Beach
I luxuriated in that sun,
seated by the dunes, aware of the halcyon sea,
idly turning the idea-less pages
of the Ideas Section of the Saturday Times
almost unaware of my luck and you.

VISITING JAPAN

The young man behind me
on the bus to Ohara, in the hills
above Kyoto, wears a sweatshirt
reading "Dreams Exciting Sweat!"
What can it mean? I'm on my way
to see a Zen priest in his temple.
I rehearse the scene. He will ask me,
What is it you want? And I will say,
to feel at home in this world.
But in his temple, where he lives alone,

a visiting Zen nun serves us lunch,
a bucket of Kentucky Fried Chicken,
which is preceded by the chanting of a sutra,
and the talk is mainly of the lack
of enlightenment among their superiors,
the Abbot in particular. Then we sit
on the porch of the temple watching
fog drift through green mountains.
The next day, in Nara, two university students,
members of a rock group called "Mushroom Salad,"
are my guides as we visit Giant Buddha
and the more beautiful buddhas, some
dating back to the 7th Century.
In the local museum, before each statue
that is also a sacred object, there is a single
white chrysanthemum in a slender vase. It seems
strange to go to a museum and then to pray there.
These people do. In the evening
for dinner at my friend Hirata's house,
we have Yosenabe made by his mother.
A large pot of broth bubbles on the table
into which she puts rice cakes, fish cakes,
vegetables, tofu, clams and clear noodles.

In a corner of the Japanese room adjoining
the Western living room in which we sit after dinner
there appears to be a Shinto shrine—
a small knee-high altar with food offerings and pictures
of relatives. A kind of shrine, my young
friend tells me. It is a homemade world
even in Japan. Rice fields
among the parking lots.

MERCY

Kuanon looks down on me from my bookshelf—
three postcard portraits, widely spaced,
on the third shelf from the top.

Purchased in Kyoto, I remember,
though I first saw her face in Tokyo
(we were introduced by Donald Richie).
I don't have to understand why she is there.
The image pleases me. She seems merciful,
and it has often been my lot to ask that of women.
I am willing to entertain the notion that
medieval Mary lurks there, but I think not:
the icon is festooned with jangling bric-a-brac.
In Kyoto I had a little guesthouse
with its own garden, sliding panels, tatami mat
and so forth. I left my shoes out in the rain
one night out of confusion. Otherwise I was fine
and at home. I also remember inviting a mama-san
from a bar in Tokyo to join me there
but she said business would not permit it.
Business rules in Japan but Kuanon is in her own space.

TOURIST IN AFRICA

In Africa, a family of baboons
even now is making the tree shake—
say it's a Kalahari apple leaf,
a pink smudge on the savannah—
and next to it an elephant
is eating his way around the bark
of an acacia. And I keep dreaming
of wart hogs, black energy and bile,
to keep me company on the open plain.

I wonder how the wart hogs are faring in Botswana,
are they keeping away from the lions,
are they still enjoying the sweet tips of the grasses,
are they moving in swart family groups silently
like a blur on the edge of the retina?

The noisome baboon befriends the gentle kudu.
You see them gamboling together
across the plain or camped together
under a giant palm. Sometimes the noisome
baboon eats the kudu's suckling young,
ripping the stomach open first
to drink the milk.

In Botswana, the ironic wart hogs
mingle with the lyrical elands.
Elephant dung beside the Cessna 200.

ISRAEL

1
In the desert
even the bare night sky
has its luminosity
as if the dark
were soaked with light.

And then the tremendous lift-off of morning.

2
Under the Romans, water
and colonnaded streets
flowed through the land
along with the blood of natives.

Stars over the Bedouin
encampments. Black tents
in black night.

The blossoms of the jacaranda tree
in morning light,
a blue scrim.

3
At the Yardenit Baptismal Site
in Galilee
blue-jeaned Scandinavian angels
change into white cotton.
As they slowly descend
the stone steps into the cool Jordan
their nipples harden.

4
In an intricate Roman mosaic floor
I see a drinking contest
between handsome Dionysus
and Heracles
(Dionysus, cup down, the winner)
and realize the goat god
would have charmed me,
when young,
to follow
through rows of cypresses
and olive trees
in his procession.

5
Sand-colored hills,
wind-wrinkled water.
An almost Mediterranean light
stiffened by terror.

6
A slag heap
ennobled by stories.

7
In Jerusalem
the crows are black,
the monks are black
and the Hasidim.
Jerusalem madness, they say,
strikes only those under thirty

with a propensity for mysticism.
Then they are seized by a belief
that they are Abraham or Sarah
or maybe Noah if the weather is bad,
sprung from the black letters of the text
into our clamorous century,
which, in truth, doesn't need
an infusion of madness
but of sanity and clarity.

8
Night in the desert.
Overhead the stars.
As on the tables of the law
those glistening tides.

HEBREW MELODIES

1
God says to Moses, "Take this down:
I will utterly blot out
the memory of Amalek."
It's in Exodus, and it's the first
reference to writing in the Bible
and His first lyric poem.

2
How odd to thank God
for watching over His people,
in the light of the evidence,
including the smoke of the 6 million.
I read all these prayers with irony.
How does the Ear receive them?

3

Elijah moored to a simple fable,
visit us this night, take in tribute
wine—from the child's eye, wine and wonder—
that the growing year, green stalk and leaf,
will see us safe and death passed over.

JERUSALEM, FOR EXAMPLE

"Life passes away—
Poetry remains."
This is what the students
of the Hebrew University Secondary School
wrote on their card to me,
handed to me
attached to a small bouquet
after my reading. I thought
they wrote it with my age in mind,
for solace. I would like to believe
that what they wrote is true.
But I know most poetry passes away,
and maybe all of my poetry will pass away
and it will be as if I had not been.
My sons may come to see my life's work
as a foolish project. When they do,
I hope they remember the happiness it gave me,
the places it took me to—
Jerusalem, for example, and my meeting with Ester,
my passing through the Lions' Gate
as if in my youth.

IT SEEMS TO ME

It seems to me that this world
is beginning to pick up speed
and is hurtling past me so quickly

that it is on the point of disappearing.
But no, I tell myself, it is I
who am picking up speed and am
almost on the point of disappearing.
This is one of those basic illusions,
e.g., the sun rising and setting,
that dizzy you when you try to dispel them
or lead you to punishing truths.

CONFESSIONS OF AGE

1
A beautiful woman says to me
"He swept me off my feet.
He sent me a dozen red roses every day."
The topic is failure, what has failed in our lives.
I want to lick up all her spilt milk.

2
I'm beginning to identify
with the babies in their strollers,
those I see in the middle of the day,
soulfully asleep.
They seem to be storing strength
for the long journey to come.

3
The day is darkening as the year is darkening.
In October the departing sun
feels like shelter.
Wondering how the American word "loneliness"
replaced the American word "sure."

1930s

I'm on a horse-drawn sleigh
in Lakewood, New Jersey,
in bright cushiony snow,
the horse jangling its way
through a deep pine forest—
breathe in, breathe in, says mother,
the air is so good—
a thick blanket over me, face to the sun.
I stay with the moment—was I five or six?—
and the universe tucks me in.

THROUGH THE RAIN

Through the rain on Sunday
on the Long Island Expressway.
Cloud upon cloud in the bus's tinted window.
I remember my dog's excitement, nose pressed
against the partially opened window
as we neared beach country—
a golden retriever who could swim forever
but is long dead. Suddenly
the green seems so rich in the divided highway.
The years all vectoring with me as I near you.

Red, green, red, green buoys.
The tide coming in from Gardiners Bay.
A shelf of thin white clouds overhead,
sound of water over sand
not the sea's loud messages.
I keep trying to figure out what to do with my life
and now it's mostly over. I've collected
poems like the shells I picked up today. I suppose
both keep some spent life in them.
I should be content with that

and with this line of trees,
blue sky showing through the burgeoning branches,
furred along the opposite shore.

The sea was playing its harmonica.
I recognized the tune.

OBSERVATIONS

When she tells a dirty joke
she is the first to roar at it,
her mouth agape, her wine-stained teeth
as beautiful as a Rembrandt or Hals.

I know it is time for final wisdom,
which is not to be found in this world,
but she distracts me, running in to tell me
news of the day, to kiss me, to make sure
I'm still anchored in this world.

What is this heavy somnolence that surrounds me
as if all the questions had been answered one by one?

Oh, to be a Nobel Laureate looking back.
How serene I would be, and with what
clarity I would view all around me,
illusion and non-illusion. And with what
justice I would pronounce judgment on my life.

LAST NIGHT'S JAZZ

I
Ancient as Chaucer
the small note words
on Louis' trumpet
when he was young

and Earl Hines was young
and the scambling life
of "West End Blues"
and "Tight Like This"
was vision in my head.

2

Mournful, ever-weeping Harlem
where we went to pick up Shorty at the funeral home
for his gig that night at Nell's on 14th Street.
Piano-playing, song-writing midget
and by day a cosmetician to corpses,
a byproduct skill from his years in vaudeville
with Stepin Fetchit. Shorty Jackson,
grinning from the keyboard, *Knock me a kiss.*

3

That's Thelonius Monk wandering
from his piano at the Five Spot
in the middle of a number.
The other members of the group
don't look up, tend to their music.
My friend Tom and I are cool, too.
We're both drifters. Tom farther.
In Austin, Texas, blue Gauloise smoke did him in.
But tonight Thelonius comes back. The Monk
comes back. He hits
just the right few notes and everybody
is together again. The crowd
in the Five Spot loves it.

THREE EPITAPHS

I bought an outmoded plot
early in life about a Poet
and his Muse, both
characters now defunct.
For a while, it was like living
in an opera. Now it's not.

The drama has gone out of
the Long Island Expressway.

A man can't fight everything
that comes through the door,
I said to Death.

HEIRLOOM

"This too shall pass"
was, I thought, a saying
of my mother's, recorded often
in my memory about almost
anything that had happened in our world.
But it was actually, now I read, inscribed
by a jeweler on a ring commissioned
by King Solomon—to temper his moods.
And that was handed down
by Solomon to my mother
and now to me.

CONFUSION AT THE WHEEL

To the broad blue sheet of Biscayne Bay
where the dead parents commingle
and maybe their last prayers for the children
still stain the lucent surface

I returned at an age older than my father's.
I am older than my father
I said to the cruising pelicans,
to the lotus eaters, to the junkies
lurking in the pink and yellow
deco palaces of Ocean Drive,
in South Beach, Miami.
Miami.
Moon over Miami. You can't die in Brooklyn,
my younger son said to me years ago,
you have to die in Miami.
I hear the waves ramping along the shore
by the dessicated palm trees,
and I think, this ocean,
this sea of time but without past,
without future, featureless, sans shape,
is my true home. Chaos is my home
and these family nostalgias,
this Miami vice, only
a quick trip to normalcy.
I remember Donald Barthelme's fable
about his real-dead father,
and Dylan Thomas' fierce father,
and my own father, confusion at the wheel.

BROOKLYN

The lights of two bridges
framed in my study window
are more pleasant to me
because more constant to me
than the ornate lit cathedral
across from my hotel in Barcelona.
Let them be my memorial candles
when I am through with this world.

EAST END

1
Wetness
like the slick of sleep
still covers. Cat blurs in.
Gulls scour
the empty reaches.
Sun's brilliance
through thin cloud hem.

2
Gulls tilting in the small waves.
Wind skirl through the rigging of a beached boat.
These scruffy bay beaches.
Suddenly sky darkens.
Wind comes up like a car.
I stay out for the pleasure
of the first rain.

Index of Titles and First Lines

ABOUT THE AUTHOR

Harvey Shapiro's many books include *How Charlie Shavers Died* (Wesleyan, 2001), *National Cold Storage Company* (Wesleyan, 1988), *The Light Holds: Poems* (Wesleyan, 1984), *This World* (Wesleyan, 1971), and *Battle Report* (Wesleyan, 1966). In 1997, Wesleyan and Carcanet co-published his *Selected Poems*. Shapiro published his first book in 1953. He taught at Cornell University and Bard College before joining the staffs of *Commentary* and *The New Yorker*. In 1957 he became an editor of *The New York Times Magazine*. He was editor of *The New York Times Book Review* from 1975 until 1983.